DON'T GIVE UP, GET UP!

This book is for:

____

Because I believe YOU are HELPful!

____

For more information, contact Heather O'Brien Walker International.

Published by Breakthrough Media Network
15 Paradise Plaza, Ste. 272
Sarasota, FL 34239
www.HeatherOBrienWalker.com | www.HELPability.com
(877) 373-2723

Printed in the United States of America.

ISBN: 978-0-9855393-4-4

DON'T GIVE UP, GET UP!

The invaluable life lessons
I learned from living in a wheelchair
and suffering two brain injuries
that will HELP you to persevere
and overcome any challenge...

BY HEATHER O'BRIEN WALKER

Praise For Don't Give Up, Get Up

"Heather's story provides more than hope. It provides HELP in the form of a powerful message that everyone should embrace. Read this book. It's well worth it."

— **Ruben Gonzalez**
4 Time Olympian

"What an incredible and inspiring story. Anyone who's experiencing struggle or wants to be better needs to read it."

— **Jason Hanson,**
Former CIA Agent
Featured on ABC's Hit TV Show "Shark Tank"

"Show me a person who has NEVER wanted to give up and I will show you they have no pulse! When you read Don't Give Up Get Up, I promise you will be inspired to persevere through any challenge."

— **Michael Dorsey,**
"Big Mike" Featured on NBC's Hit TV Show "The Biggest Loser"

"As Director of the Napoleon HIll foundation, I have traveled around the world and have seen many amazing speakers. Heather's talk inspires you to take action, which is one of Napoleon Hill's keys to achieving success in anything you do."

— **Don Green,**
Napoleon Hill Foundation, Executive Director

"Heather O'Brien Walker is an inspiration in every sense of the word. This book is a must read for anyone who wants to rise above the challenges of life to live their best, feel their best and be their best!"

— **Julie Marie Carrier,**
MissVirginia USA 2002
Teen Coach on MTV's Hit TV Show, "MADE"

"By developing a championship mindset you can soar amongst the clouds and make a difference in the world. Read this book for a new and better you."

— **Kory Minor,**
Former NFL Linebacker,
University of Notre Dame
All-American & Captain

"As a two-time Olympian, my journey to health would have been much easier if I had known and applied Heather's HELP philosophy. She defines a pathway to overcoming obstacles and sustaining an attitude of success throughout the journey."

— **Sherry M. Winn,**
2 Time Olympian
National Championship Coach

"We all get down but Heather gives us the hope, the encouragement and the plan for getting back up, whether it's a setback, a disappointment, a loss, or an injury!"

— **James Wanless,**
Ph.D. Columbia University

"Heather's story is simply amazing and her HELP philosophy is great. Heather will inspire many to live their dreams!"

— **Barbara Niven**
Top Media Trainer, featured in over 100 film and TV roles, and a regular on the Lifetime Channel

"Heather is a shining example of inspiration and brilliance! She is an incredible example of someone who overcame serious adversity, and what she teaches will provide a beacon of hope and direction!"

— **Steven R. Shallenberger**
Key Designer of the World-Renowned Covey Planner
Founder Becoming Your Best Global Leadership LLC

"What an inspiration! Heather has lived the life of a Rhino, getting knocked down, but always rising to charge ahead. A definite must read for anyone facing difficulties that seem insurmountable."

— **Scott Alexander,**
Author of the Classic Rhinoceros Success
with NY Times Best Seller, Dave Ramsey

"No matter what obstacle you are facing in your life, this book can HELP you! Heather brings a fresh perspective from her injuries and experiences giving you a renewed power and strength to Get UP!"

— **Elizabeth McCormick,**
Former US Army Black Hawk Pilot

"The message in this book inspired me to do more and be more. Heather is a living, walking example of an amazing woman who walks her talk."

— **Jill Lublin,**
Author of Guerrilla Publicity

"This book needs to be shared with as many people as possible! Heather's story and her philosophy on how anyone can overcome and achieve success is remarkable. I highly recommend it."

— **Bill Bartmann**
Billionaire Entrepreneur and Author

"This is an amazing and unbelievable story of courage. I am a believer in visualization. Your determination, positive attitude, and mental movie to walk again despite all the odds is so inspiring!"

— **Sara Blakely**
Founder of Spanx, and the world's youngest self-made female billionaire

"Overcoming adversity and life's most challenging problems is the hallmark of success. Most people live frustrating lives as victims rather than living a victorious life of accomplishment. Heather's remarkable life story will inspire anyone to never give up."

— **Dave Anderson "America's Rib King", Founder of Famous Dave's BBQ Restaurant chain**
(190 Restaurants & $500 Million in Revenue)

Speaking

Heather is featured featured New York Times Best Seller, Lifestyle Coach, and highly sought after inspirational speaker who can speak for crowds ranging from 20 to 20,000. Sharing her unique, signature presentation, "Don't Give Up – Get Up!" as well as her "HELPability® Factor" presentation based on her second book of the same name, she inspires people around the world.

Heather is a proud member of the International Positive Psychology Association and bases her teachings on personal experiences, certifications and evidence-based research in positive psychology from Harvard University.

Audiences and clients love Heather's message because it's backed up with leading-edge theory and evidence. It includes a simple 5-step process she helps them implement right away, geared toward helping them discover all that life can be.

Heather shares the benefits of positive emotions on the heart and immune system, and how to use her system to always be in a state of positive attraction.

Heather is available to speak for variety of audiences...corporations, business groups, associations, colleges, universities, youth groups, community groups and sports organizations.

Any organization looking for a speaker who will inspire their audience to overcome adversity and achieve greater success in life and business needs to hire Heather for a keynote and/or workshop training.

For booking fees and details, please contact:

Heather O'Brien Walker International
15 Paradise Plaza, Ste. 272
Sarasota, FL 34239

Email:

heather@helpability.com

Web:

www.HELPability.com |
www.HeatherOBrienWalker.com

Toll Free:

(877) 373-2723

Special Sales

Don't Give Up, Get Up™ is available at special discounts for bulk purchases, sales promotions, premiums, and giveaways. Special editions, including personalized covers, excerpts from existing books, and customized and corporate imprints can be produced in larger quantities for your special needs.

For more information, please contact
heather@helpability.com, or call (877) 373-2723

Acknowledgments

With deep gratitude I would like to thank my husband, **TW Walker** to whom I literally owe my life today as I know it. Even though we weren't married at the time, you stood by me and nurtured my healing better than any husband I could have imagined. You never saw me as broken or damaged, but simply the woman you fell in love with; that simple act was the most potent healing remedy I have ever received.

To my parents **Mary Ann and Tom O'Brien** thank you for always being there for me, and for showing me that the love a family has is forever in our hearts.

To my sister **Dru O'Brien** thank you for the all the healing laughter and special sharing over the years, that only sisters can know.

To my aunt **Julia O'Brien** who now lives in heaven, thank you for teaching me about the Angels and how to listen to their messages. You are my shining example of how to live.

To my aunt **Carol Mc Laughlin** thank you, for showing me the artistry of makeup and that an aunt can be a very special friend, too.

To my special friend **Wizard** who showed me that unconditional love came in a fuzzy gray and white package, you will forever be in my heart.

To my friend **Jill Obrachta** thank you for always being my soul sister and for your steadfast support when I was injured and trying to plan a wedding. You are what true friends are made of.

To my friend **Jodi Blattert** thank you for a lifelong friendship that seems to never miss a beat, no matter how much time has passed. There is a true comfort in a childhood friendship.

To my physical therapists **David Griffith and Anita Gerbig** thank you for believing in me when I was so afraid. I credit you both for getting me up, literally and walking again. The care and concern you gave me far exceed any job description.

To my doctor **Dr. Martha Huie** thank you for helping to me to remember the person I was before my accidents and assuring me that all that mattered was my heart was still the same.

To my friend **David Childerly** you were a lifeline in my darkest hour and I thank you for helping me to dream again.

To my friend **Barbara Niven** thank you for being a shining example of "Star Power" and lighting the way for me.

To **Scott Bell** the brother that I never had, thank you for your wonderful friendship and faith in me over the years.

To my **Elysian Fields Family** thank you for being my classroom full of extraordinary women who showed me that love, kindness and grace comes from an open heart.

To my new friend **LaVonna Roth** thank you for recognizing me and embracing me as one of your family.

To **Jack Canfield** thank you for showing me the power of the wonderful art of visualization that helped me to walk again. Also, for sharing my story in your New York Times Best Seller 'The Success Principles' - 10th Anniversary Edition. Truly a dream come true.

To **Helen Gerro** thank you for making my amazing wedding and speaking dresses. You are one of a kind, just like them.

And last but certainly not least, thank you to my dear friend, confidant and editor **Valarie Clark** who pulled everything together and turned this idea for a book that was rolling around in my head into a reality.

TW and I two months after our engagement.
Having a great time in St. Maraten.

Dedication

I would not be the person I am today without the unyielding support, respect and belief of my husband TW Walker. So, from the depths of my heart I dedicate this book to you.

When I couldn't see, you guided me with your strong arms. When I stumbled and fell, you picked me up time and time again. When I cried in pain and fear you comforted me. When I told you I wanted to tell my story, you believed in me.

To my number one fan, words cannot convey my gratitude for helping me put the pieces back together better than I could have imagined.

My first steps as a Walker with TW. I had achieved my goal!

Foreword

Barbara Niven

Top Media Trainer, Appeared in over 100 film and TV roles and 2500 TV & radio commercials.

Heather O'Brien Walker is amazing. She is one of those beautiful people who shines from the inside out. Happy. Gorgeous. Loving. Giving.

Looking at her, you'd never guess she'd ever had a problem in her life. But that's why her story is so important. The unthinkable did happen to her. She suffered devastating, traumatic brain injuries. Twice. Yet she didn't wallow in pity, and she didn't let it define her. She fought back with a warrior's mindset and spirit and reclaimed her life, far surpassing the doctors' wildest projections.

Heather is the definition of courage and success, and her story is the stuff of Hollywood movies. She will inspire and empower you to never give up, but to simply get up and try again.

Coming back from a brain injury is not easy. She had to relearn even the simplest things we take for granted: talking, standing, walking, even new ways of "thinking" as her brain tried to heal. With her loving husband, TW, at her side every step of the way, she finally went from being wheelchair-bound to walking down the aisle on her wedding day.

During this struggle, Heather developed tools that helped her systematically reclaim her life, to not only survive, but thrive! She calls this system HELPability® and her HELP philosophy®, "HELP: Hope, Encouragement, Love and Positivity." She shares it now to help others achieve their own dreams and goals, and is a powerful motivational speaker.

Thank you, Heather. You inspire me every day, and I am proud to call you friend.

– **Barbara Niven**
Actress, Media Trainer, Speaker, Author

Preface

What are the odds of sustaining two brain injuries within 40 days? That's just what happened to Heather O'Brien Walker in 2011. She wasn't jumping out of airplanes or living in a war zone or playing a professional contact sport...she was just like you.

On the afternoon of July 29th 2011, Heather was going about her day as an executive at a luxury retailer. Making her way to her office, she fell over a box left carelessly in a walkway, striking her head and altering her life's course forever. Found unconscious and unresponsive by fellow employees, Heather was transported via helicopter to a nearby trauma center where she was diagnosed with a traumatic brain injury. Disoriented and unable to communicate or walk, Heather endured a week of evaluations; her fiancé TW never left her side.

Heather was released from the trauma hospital and transferred to a rehabilitation hospital where she spent weeks confined to a wheelchair learning how to do the most basic tasks; brush her teeth, raise a fork to her mouth, speak clearly. Doctors warned she would most likely never be completely free of the vast array of symptoms common to sufferers of traumatic brain trauma.

One month later, Heather was finally released to the full time care of TW. One week after leaving the rehabilitation hospital, Heather and TW, on their way home from a doctor's appointment, were involved in a 40 mph collision with a reckless driver. Heather's side of the vehicle took the brunt of the impact and she sustained a second traumatic brain injury, losing all the headway she had gained during her rehabilitation and also suffering a host of new injuries. Her fiancé, TW was also injured, requiring multiple surgeries.

In a matter of months, Heather had gone from ecstatic bride-to-be with a glamorous new job and nothing but blue skies ahead to a young woman confined to a wheelchair, dependent on the man she loved for the simplest daily needs. It was during these darkest days that Heather manifested her HELP philosophy®.

Heather and TW relied on HELP (Hope, Encouragement, Love and Positivity) to sustain them during their many struggles to regain their health and emotional strength; they knew it was crucial to have faith in HELP to overcome all they faced.

Using the HELP philosophy®, in spite of overwhelming injuries and life circumstances, they set their wedding date and were boldly determined that Heather would walk down the aisle unassisted. They sensed they would need a miracle; they sensed through HELP and faith, that they would indeed get onc.

On April 14, 2012, seven months after sustaining her second brain injury, Heather and TW were married in a beautiful beach wedding ceremony. Like a mermaid who had found her legs, Heather walked down the aisle unassisted.

Learn how this amazing couple took steps to overcome the many obstacles they faced, dealing not only with their injuries and long recoveries, but all the overwhelming challenges life presented. Read their inspirational story of the many miraculous things they have experienced. Learn how to apply strategies in your life that will enable you to feel powerful even under the most daunting of challenges using the HELP philosophy®.

Table Of Contents

INTRODUCTION

"A champion is someone who gets up when he can't."
—Jack Dempsey

Heather's Journal Entry: August 23, 2011

"I don't know why this is all happening right now. I guess I may never know. I am so scared, but still, deep inside I feel a sense something good is coming."

Someone was calling my name; from far away at first but getting louder. I don't want to get up yet. That voice! Why is my mother trying to wake me? Do I have to get up to go to school? I want to bury my head under the covers and sleep; just sleep.

Heather… Heather...

I wish she would leave me alone; I'm so tired and sick – my mouth – watery – so dizzy, violent waves of nausea. Open my eyes! I must open my eyes! They won't budge. I manage to peer through tiny slits, the room is so shockingly bright it burns my eyes. I can make out only blurry images.

The surface on which I lie is cold and hard, I have a death grip on vast cold flatness. And that voice! No! Now, many voices!

Heather…Heather!

The flat surface begins to spin, like an amusement park ride, turning and lurching in all directions. If I loosen my grasp even a little I will fall away into the nothingness.

What is happening? Where am I? I'm not in my bed. My mother is not here?

It is a struggle to sit up, as if there is a bolder on my chest. My head throbs with a thunder; which is upstaged only by a skull-crushing pressure. And that piercing ring! Someone, please make it stop! My ears! Please! It is so loud! Help me!

Please? Someone? Anyone?

I am awake! The pain is excruciating; a hot sear shooting through my body, my skin feels as if it is on fire. Again, I attempt to sit up – why is it so difficult? Then it hit me – my legs will not move!

"Heather..."

Thank goodness! TW, is standing next to me. His expression is one of relief and fear. He stroked my hair. "It's okay. I'm with you. I'm right here."

"Wwwhhhaaett?" I pleaded with him to tell me what was going on but all that came out between my river of tears and gulps of breath was a garbled croaking sound.

"WWWWHHHAAAEEETTT?" What was wrong with me?

I tried again to say something else to TW and another weird sound came out; something that resembled a mix between Chewbacca and E.T.

This can't be real. This is the strangest nightmare ever.

"You have had an accident. You tripped and hit your head." TW continued to stroke my hair as I tried to understand what his words meant.

Accident? I had an accident? How could I be in an accident, I was just laying in my bed?

He must be joking with me, as he usually does. So I waited for the punch line to come from him. I wanted a punch line NOW, more than ever.

"You fell at work. They brought you here in a helicopter. You're in a hospital."

What are you talking about? I was stymied. I was just in bed and my Mom was here trying to get me up. Helicopter? What's a helicopter? That's a really funny word. Helicopter? Helicopter, helicopter...I wonder what it means?

My mind got stuck on that word like a video that plays the same section over and over again. Helicopter...Helicopter...

A smiling woman came over to the bed and patted my arm. She gently checked me over and for the first time I noticed the IV in my hand and almost passed out. Needles! I'm on an IV? What?

The nurse flashed a light into my eyes and began talking very fast.

Oh God, please stop that, please stop that right now! What in the world are you doing? I could barely stand the light.

I couldn't recognize all her words either. I had to try to concentrate really hard to figure out what the words meant, and then what they meant altogether.

She tried again. Smiling and slower this time she said, "I have a few questions for you. What's your name?"

I turned my head towards her to reply; confident I knew the answer but before I could croak out my name, a huge wave of nausea hit me and I sent vomit hurling in her direction.

Oh no! That wasn't good. That wasn't good at all!

Even in my dazed and confused state I was so embarrassed. I certainly don't throw up on people! She took it in stride and quickly turned to get something to clean us both up.

I noticed a clear bag near my feet.

I asked TW, "WWWHHHHAAATTT TTTHHHAATTTT?"

He glanced down at the bag and then looked back at me with a pained look on his face.

"You don't want to know."

That didn't sound good. I asked more emphatically this time, "WWWWHHHAAAATTTTT...?"

"It's your clothes...the pieces of the suit you had on," he said in a low tone of voice.

It took a while to register what that meant. Then it hit me, he had said 'the pieces.' The pieces? My brand new Chanel suit was in pieces? I started to cry much harder realizing that I had only worn my suit for a few short hours and now it was in PIECES.

Suddenly, my body's alert system went into overdrive and I was really feeling the full effects the fall. My body began reacting as if it were under attack – the spasms came on like gangbusters – I shook involuntarily from head to toe. All I could do was look at TW with what must have been a "deer in the headlights" expression. He just talked softly to me and said, "Everything is going to be alright."

I wanted to believe him more than anything in the world. But, as I became more and more aware of what was happening, it became more difficult to hang onto hope. I hadn't been this frightened in a very long time.

TW took my cold hand as it trembled and placed it in his warm, strong hand and whispered into my ear, "Heather, we can do this. You are going to get through this. I'm not going anywhere; I love you. You will be fine. We will be fine. I'm positive." TW gave me everything right there in that a sentence; hope, encouragement, love and the knowing that we would begin right then and there to move forward together. I managed to squeeze his hand in response; it wasn't much but it was everything I had.

When the nurse returned she was pleasant and reassuring and tried to calm me. She had a way about her that was very efficient but also gentle as she wiped the vomit from my gown. There was another woman in the room. She had a mop and was humming a little tune as she worked her magic on the floor. Although the sound of her hum hurt my ears there was also something soothing about her voice.

Vomit gone and order restored, the nurse returned to the matter at hand. "Do you know where you are?"

"Hossptll?" I was able to croak out something that resembled the word hospital.

The line between her eyebrows furrowed with concern. "Who is the president of the United States?"

I took a long pause. A very clear picture appeared in my head: a tall man with dark hair and A MONKEY; Ronald Reagan!

"Rrrrrrrruuuunnnnaaallldddd AAAAAgggggaaaannnnn!" A deeper furrow formed between my nurse's brow. I looked over to TW who for one second was the smiling laughing man I fell in love with and in the next became the man who realized a terrifying trip had just been booked for the two of us.

Dear (Your Name Here),

The year was 2011 and the President was Barack Obama when the nurse asked me who the president was at that time. Little did I realize but a simple brown cardboard box had changed my life. As a result of the fall my brain was stuck in the 80s. Boxes can hold trash or they can hold treasures and as difficult as it was going to be my brown box had given me the gift of choice. I could have fallen victim to my circumstances and stayed stuck in my wheelchair or I could choose to work hard to regain my physical health and independence. I could choose to give up and remain helpless or I could choose to get up and claim being helpful.

Which do you want? Do you choose to be less or do you choose to be full? What is in your brown box? Let me ask you, when was the last time you were tripped up in your life or your business? Things were going along great and then BAM! A challenge you never saw coming packs a punch and lays you out on the floor like a washed up prizefighter. How did that make you feel? Did you feel helpless or powerless? Did it make you feel as if you had no control over your life?

Did you allow circumstance to take the driver's seat and drag you along by the bumper? Did you feel in the pit of your stomach that things were being done to you and you had no say in the matter? Did negative thoughts get all balled up together and roll downhill getting bigger and bigger? What if I don't reach my life goals? Will I get to the end and be disappointed with the way my life turned out? Did I not take enough risks? Take enough time to feel joy? Did I do enough? Did I love enough?

If you've had any of these fears, asked any of these questions, trust me I know just how you feel. My accidents took me on that exact journey – I've rolled down that hill – and I was afraid, very afraid. I am no different than you.

However, I managed to learn some very tough lessons during that experience; I learned how to gain mastery of my power even in the midst of a chaos spiral. I want to share what I learned with you. You will see me refer to help a lot in this book; for me, HELP means: Hope, Encouragement, Love and Positivity; every time I see the word HELP I do an immediate self check to see if I am feeling HELPful or HELPless. If the answer is helpless I begin to look outside myself and around my world to see where the need is; how I can be of service to others and Be HELPful to them. You see, to fill a need in another is to fill a hole in oneself.

Therapy trip to the beach on Anna Maria Island Florida.
I wanted more than anything to walk in the sand.

CHAPTER ONE

YOU AND ME

This Book Will Meet You Right Where You Are

"One of the most common causes of failure is the habit of quitting when one is overtaken by temporary defeat."
—Napoleon Hill

Heather's Journal Entry: September 12, 2011

"Realizing that no matter what I am facing I can always be HELPFUL to others, was one of those moments when the light bulb goes off and I finally "got it". It was kind of like Dorothy in Oz having the power to go home all the time but she had to take the journey to realize that she had that power all along."

My name is Heather O'Brien Walker and I am the thriver-survivor of two catastrophic back injuries, a near-death experience and two traumatic brain injuries. I would like to share with you my core philosophy for healing, thriving and surviving trauma and or life-altering challenges. It is my wish that my HELP Philosophy will support you on your own journey from feelings of helplessness to helpfulness.

In November of 2011, I attended a speaking event with my then fiancé, TW. Wheel-chair bound, still in recovery from my most recent traumatic brain injury, unable to take care of my most basic needs, I listened closely to a speaker as he talked with the audience about the power of shared experiences. He explained how our obstacles, our traumas, our crises, our journeys can be used to inspire, teach and motivate others who are in the midst of their own journey. How people learn the most precious lessons from these experiences and use it to further their lives. He then explained how it was possible to share my story through public speaking and therefore become more helpful in the world and be of service to others.

During the seminar, as I sat there in my wheelchair, a realization swept through me like a rush of morphine. I turned to TW and whispered,

"This is it! This is what I am supposed to be doing!"

Despite knowing that I couldn't yet walk, speak clearly, or even bathe myself, TW smiled at me and said, "I believe in you."

Now married to TW, who is my biggest supporter and number one fan, I share my HELP Philosophy® and HELPability® system with others from around the world as I continue to heal and learn new ways to serve and Be HELPful.

Immediately, from the first time I heard this man speak, I set two goals for myself: embrace the power of public speaking and put my story on paper. The later has proved to be a bit of a struggle for me as daily I contend with the aftermath of the brain injuries. It was a conversation with a new friend, Jerome Carter, who is also a beautiful writer and minister among other things, that spurred me on to complete my goal.

After sharing some of my story with Jerome he asked me, "Why are you being so selfish?" Me? Selfish? I was so struck by his question. Yet, his fantastic smile and the warmth in his eyes told me he meant no ill will. He went on to share with me one of his most beautiful poems, **The World Is Waiting For Your Gift**. I was so moved by his message that it was there and then I made a commitment to not wait another minute to share the gift of story in a book for you, with the hope that you can travel from helplessness to helpfulness and live a thriver-surviver life.

The World Is Waiting For Your Gift

The world is waiting for your gift
So don't be selfish, share it and give society a lift

Don't be paralyzed by criticism or fear
You must understand, someone's life
Will be enhanced because you are here!

We all have special talents that we are blessed with from birth
To share, give and help others as we journey through our planet earth

You have so much to offer this community
Whether it's artistic, writing a book or producing a CD

So, what are you waiting for?
Please don't procrastinate anymore
The world is waiting there is so much in store

Please don't say I will wait till next year
Then you cheat the world for another 12 months my dear!
Don't let the thought of success or failure grip you with fear

Give your gift to the world and we'll celebrate and have a toast
You can make a difference or make excuses but you can't do both

It's time to prioritize, start the process and go down the list
Let the journey begin, because the world is waiting for your gift!
"No one can give your gift but you, it's time to present the present!"
Jerome Vincent Carter

Inspiration 52: *The Blueprint For Greatness*
www.inspiration52.org

Jerome and I after our "selfish" conversation.
He changed my whole perspective with one word.

However this book has found you, perhaps you have heard me speak to your group or being interviewed on the radio. Maybe you purchased a copy for yourself or were given one by a friend, or one was provided to you at an event or by your company. Whatever the case, you have made the choice to open it and receive my message. It is my hope that what I present here will be of some HELP to you in your life. I believe that this book has found you, as it was meant to; in this very moment, as you stand there with your life looking just the way it does, for a reason. You are the only person that knows that reason. You may not know what the reason is just yet; perhaps it will be revealed to you at a later time. Consider that there is a reason why you are here with me now. The choices you have made in the past have brought you here in the present.

There are a few things I want to share with you before we really dig in. This book is going to be a very personal conversation between you and me. This is going to be the kind of conversation that takes place between two close friends. I am going to share with you an intimate look into my personal struggles and challenges in the hope that you will gain insight from the lessons I have learned.

One of my mentors, the amazing speaker and author Jonathan Sprinkles, has a philosophy that says you can't really hear someone until you know them. It is important that you know some things about me before we begin this journey together. It's vital that you really hear me because I have faith that my HELP Philosophy ® will help you the next time you are faced with a challenge and believe me it will come – be prepared for it!

The great father of the modern success movement, Napoleon Hill, calls a persons WHY their burning desire. I think that one of the best ways to really get to know someone quickly is to discover through inquiry WHY they do the things they do; WHY they believe the things they believe; WHY they get up in the morning; WHY they make sacrifices; WHY they chose their career; WHY they decided to have children or not to have children; WHY do they go on with life? What is driving their life force – you have to know their WHY. I always ask WHY someone has attended a conference when I am doing a book signing or taking pictures with attendees, to get a quick glimpse into who they are.

What's my WHY for writing this book and what's in it for you? I wrote this book first and foremost to share with you how I used my HELP Philosophy ® to face my particular circumstances and how you can apply it in your life. If just one person finds this book HELPful, all the experiences I have had will be well worth the journey.

After that first seminar I was so inspired to share my story and help others that I started writing the manuscript that would become this book. A year and a half would pass before the final product was completed, but my husband, TW continued to be my biggest supporter and number one fan. He believed in me during those days where I struggled to heal and learn a whole new way of thinking about my life. I admit that those were some of the most difficult days I have ever experienced, because I knew what

I was meant to do but whether it was my brain injuries or simply my own fears, progress on it was slower than I wanted.

Although I loved to write and have done so throughout my career and for myself personally, I struggled. What I did manage to do is read veraciously and take notes on anything that I thought would be helpful to me later in writing my book. A quote here, an idea there, I would journal them all down...for later. The progress of putting my book together was painstakingly slow until that dinner with my friend Jerome Carter. I guess it is true: when the student is ready the teacher will come! The world *is* waiting for our gifts – we all have them to share; what was I waiting for?

I was so moved by Jerome's message that it was then and there I made a commitment to not wait another minute to share my gift of how to have mastery over challenge; the date was July 29th 2013, two years to the day of my first brain injury

Let's face it, it can be tough for anyone to put a book together, let alone someone with two brain injuries. There are times when things are more difficult for me than others, so I had to write whenever I was "in my right mind." A lot of the time my focus jumps around like a five-year-old on top of a mattress; perhaps you know that feeling. For instance you are trying to write that email and the dog is barking, you're thinking about what to fix for dinner then you remember you that you have to put that shirt in the wash for tomorrow and then that song drops into your head "Tomorrow, tomorrow, I love ya tomorrow. You're only a day a way..." Having a brain injury is like making coffee with no filter. You put the coffee and the water in the machine, but without a filter what comes out is a big ole mess!

I still deal with a ton of symptoms and life changes from my brain injuries. I run into doors, tables, couches. I have the bruises to prove it. I tell you this because I want nothing more than to be real with you; to show you that no matter what you are facing right now, you don't have to be perfect or completely healed to jump on the bus to your future. You can accomplish your goals and help others; you can move forward not only despite your wounds but because of them.

It was a huge challenge for me to go back and retell my personal stories. Who wants to share their failures and mistakes? I tell the stories because I care about you and I want you to benefit from what I have learned. My hope is that if you see how I weathered my challenges and despite the odds am now able to write books and to speak to inspire others, than you can see yourself accomplishing your goals as well.

I had some concern telling a story that involved so many other people. I care about these people and people in general and I didn't want to do anything that would hurt them. Then, I realized my story had nothing to do with them, my story has everything to do with me alone. The only person in the world with my perspective is me. I am the only one looking out through my eyes: tell your own story.

I also want to state that everything I have included here is based upon my own personal experience and research. I'm not a medical doctor nor have I had any medical training whatsoever. If you have a medical concern please investigate your particular situation with your medical professional.

The legendary Zig Ziglar said, "You can have everything in life that you want, if you just give enough other people what they want." What I hope to give you in this book, is a new perspective in which to view challenges in your life and the tools to overcome them. My mission is to teach you how to go from responding to your life challenges from a place of helplessness, to a much more powerful helpful response. This book will meet you right where you are, no matter what your life looks like. It is my mission to show people how to get up and take the first step – always the most difficult – from feeling HELPless in a challenging situation to feeling HELPful. What I personally hope to get out of sharing this story with you is to be HELPful on a global scale. I am HELPful to you and in return I ask you to Be HELPful to someone else and they in turn are HELPful to another. And so it goes. We can make an impact in this world together.

Anyone can use the HELP Philosophy® no matter where you live, how old you are, if you are a man or woman, no matter the depth or breadth of the river you must cross. We all have challenges to varying degrees and we all experience them differently. Your gift lies not in the experience of the challenge but in your response to the challenge.

This book is about sharing with you the tools and strategies I used to overcome life-threatening and life-changing circumstances. It is about revealing the proven philosophy I use to this day, that arose out of adversity that threatened my very existence, as I knew it.

We have made thousands upon thousands of choices every single moment of every day, from the first second we had the realization that we actually had different options to choose from. Over the years as we became more and more independent of our parents and responsible for our lives, the choices grew to colossal proportions. Everything from the basic decision of when we get up in the morning to how we will invest our allotment of precious time given to us every day is our choice. All of our choices form the routines and habits that culminate into the life we have today. We eventually get to the point where we don't even realize we are making choices, because our mind simply goes to the choice we have made 1000 times before.

Through the years I have been presented with many life variables where I felt as though my life choices had been taken away from me. When I was bullied as a child and went to adults for help and when their help was not enough to make it stop, I made an unconscious choice to be brave, to do well in school and not let the bullies define me. When a fall down the stairwell at my dorm rendered me physically helpless and dependent on the expertise of my doctors, I made the very conscious choice to have a surgery that would ultimately put me back on my feet. When my first husband stole my money and ended our marriage on a Christmas day many years ago, I made a choice that his behavior would not establish my own going forward. When I tripped over that box in the walkway at my new job and was involved in a car accident only 40 days after the first accident and sustained two brain injuries, I couldn't walk, talk, or function as an adult. I chose to work my butt off in physical therapy, to seek alternative healing modalities and ultimately to create a new life, a better one than before the accident.

One moment we are all going about our daily lives and in the next some of us will have our lives altered temporarily or permanently; neither outcome has to be life- defeating. When the life-altering events happened in my life, for a time I felt as my choices had been stolen from me; however just as the pain in my back moved me towards life-enhancing surgery, the pain of remaining helpless and dependent helped to lift me to new heights of relief-seeking behaviors. Being unable to walk inspired me to turn off my decision making automatic pilot. I began to see that I had choices. I came to realize that no matter what state I was in, if I was conscious, I had choices. I would walk and talk again.

Choices are where our real power lies. When we are faced with a challenging situation, such as the loss of a job or a home, the death of a spouse or family member, the end of a relationship, an auto accident, a devastating health diagnosis, we can view ourselves as either helpless or hopeful. Hope loosens up our perceptions to lean towards the idea of choices. I am a living example of no matter what trial you are facing there are always choices to be made. The simple of act of choosing is a tool for empowerment. Remember: You always have a choice in how you choose to respond to any challenge. No one can take choice away from you but you.

The great teacher Iyanla Vanzant, who has been a huge influence in my life, has this to say about choice and opportunity:

"At every single moment, we are given the opportunity to choose our future. What we do today will determine what we face next week, next month, or next year. It is the moment of a particular occurrence that we are called upon to make a choice: Will I do it the way I've always done it, or will I do it a different way."

As you read through my personal history of "particular occurrences" you will see choices I was presented with and the choices I made. Did I choose wisely every time? The answer is a resounding NO! But, I learned as I faced my challenges that I always had the power of choice, which was helpful in so many ways. And, that by not choosing was indeed making a choice as well, which in most cases leaves one feeling helpless.

I don't know about you, but I'm a big fan of "full" as opposed to "less." It was when I was in the hospital feeling quite helpless that I began to mull the word "HELPful" around in my head. Helpful is defined as:

> Providing assistance; useful.
>
> Serving a useful function; giving help.
>
> Giving or rendering aid or assistance; being of service.

Meditate on this definition, consider deeply the meaning, the fullness of being helpful. Giving! Aid! Assistance! Useful! All positive, strong, empowering traits that I decided to master and develop as my personal philosophy for an enhanced life that is full, not less. These tenets are the foundation of my HELP Philosophy® and what HELPability® is all about.

Hope – Belief in Good Outcomes

Encouragement – Inspire with Courage

Love – Passionate Affection

Positivity – Moving in a Beneficial Direction

Choices are where our real power lies. Choose HELP. When you are faced with a challenging situation, like the loss of a job or a home, or a health concern for you or a loved one, choose HELPful over HELPless. I am here to tell you that no matter what you are facing, *YOU ALWAYS HAVE A CHOICE IN HOW YOU RESPOND TO ANY DIFFICULTY AND THE FREEDOM OF CHOICE ITSELF IS EMPOWERING.*

I still get overwhelmed and bump into things and drop stuff and say the wrong word, but I've learned as I face my challenges that I always have the power of choosing to be HELPful. Trust me, remaining helpless is a recipe for disaster in your life. Your resentment and self-pity will build to epic proportions and you will find yourself in a hole you may never be able to climb out from.

Understandably, some of you may be in circumstances so dire at this time you can't see your way clear to tomorrow without wanting to kill someone or die yourself. You may be thinking that I have hit my head one too many times and that I must be crazy! All this helpful-positivity talk isn't for you! Your house is being foreclosed on and your spouse just lost his or her job. Your child has just been diagnosed with cystic fibrosis or your elderly mother with Alzheimer's. You may have rheumatoid arthritis and the simple act of turning these pages has been painful at best. You may be wondering how in the world can I be asking you to be the HELPful one? It's you that needs the help! Please believe me when I say to you that the single most beneficiary path to healing, calmness or grace in adversity is reaching out to others with any single tenet of the HELPful Philosophy®. By giving you will receive.

How do I know this? Because I felt helpless in my conditions during each physical trauma; what I mean by helpless is that I felt completely void of hope, encouragement, love and positvity. Keep in mind, I had plenty of support around me in the form of family, friends and medical staff, but I still felt helpless and I couldn't at first understand why. Then I figured it out: Everyone around me – including me – was focused on all of the things that were wrong with me; everyone was so sorry about my situation; with all the negative focus, how could I expect anything positive to come forth through the dark shadow of doom? I had to find a way to restore hope, encouragement, love and positivity to my life in order to once again feel powerful and feel helpful as opposed to helpless.

Believe in good outcomes! Inspire with courage! Display passionate affection! Move in beneficial directions!

Jonathan Sprinkles and I having fun and sending a text picture to TW.
This was the first time I traveled by myself since the accident.

CHAPTER TWO

HOPE

Belief In Good Outcomes

"Everything that is done in the world is done by hope."
—Martin Luther

Heather's Journal Entry: August 24, 2011

"I need to remember to always have a little hope tucked away in my heart when I am feeling my most desperate and I know I will continue to persevere. I have learned it's best to have hope about something unrelated to my condition and me. Something that's easy to love, like nature. I have hope that I will experience a breathtaking sunset tonight, and I will do it with enthusiasm. Sunsets are ever changing, but they are always beautiful."

Unfortunately, challenges don't come with warning labels. You simply turn around and you get clocked. You arrive at your office on Monday morning to a pink slip on your desk. Your blood tests come back with some suspicious findings. Your spouse tells you they're just not happy anymore. Your biggest client just declared bankruptcy.

Your elderly mother is diagnosed with Alzheimer's. Your new supervisor just screamed at you in front of your staff. Your identity is stolen and your credit is ruined.

I know you have been there. We all have. And if you haven't, know that your time is coming. Everyone gets a turn, no matter who you are.

If you've been there, how did you respond when the blow hit you right between the eyes? Did you cry? Did you get mad? Did you just feel like crawling in a hole and pulling the dirt in over you? How ever you answered those questions know that all of those responses are perfectly normal and understandable. We will do anything to avoid dealing with pain; we seldom have perfected our coping skills.

We can't go through life thinking these calamities only happen to the other guy and blindly go about our business. No! Just like we prepare for a hurricane or a blizzard, we must have a plan of action in place to respond to life storms as well; the time for preparation is now, not when we find ourselves in the middle of it.

Unlike our ancestors who put up food for the winter, stored a loaded rifle by the door and could build a fire from sticks, we are now a society of putting out fires instead of starting controlled burns designed to minimize damage. We don't plan ahead for personal disaster; we don't shore up our emotional reserves. That is until someone or something makes us rethink our method of "business as usual." That is part of what I am here to do.

The reverse is also true; we can be over-prepared, living a life of hypervigilance; always waiting for the other shoe to drop, a door to slam in our face, a phone call to deliver devastating news. Living our lives on the defense leaves little time to enjoy life. So what should you do? How should you prepare?

Difficult times will arrive in your life unexpectedly and the way I have found to feel HELPful rather than HELPless during these times is to believe that when this particular chapter of your life is finished you will be happy with the closing remarks. No matter what may come you have to have belief that a good outcome is possible.

July 29th 2011 started out no more remarkable than any other day. Well, except for that I was wearing a *new* Chanel suit. And, I was just a few weeks into my new job at Swankiest Store

Ever. Executive position. Uh huh! My cell phone alerted me to an incoming call as I buzzed along the morning-lit streets of Sarasota Florida. Jill!

"Hey Jilly Bean!"

"Morning Girly Girl! We are still on for dinner tonight, yes?" Jill sounded as excited as I felt.

"You betchya!" I couldn't wait for our dinner meeting. We were going to go over wedding ideas. My friend Jill was so fantastic at putting together occasions and taking care of details.

"Oh good! I am super excited to go over all your wedding ideas and, drum roll please, start figuring out the dress!"

"I know, right? That's the one thing that really makes it real, when you find the perfect dress. That's when you really feel like a bride. Well, the perfect dress *and* the perfect man! I can hardly believe I am actually getting married! This last year or so has been a whirlwind. Europe. Tahiti. Now, here - Sarasota. I am happy to be settling down."

"I know. I am so glad that the distance didn't come between us. Thank God for technology. I could talk to you just like you were down the street. By the way how is TW?"

"He's really good. I think he is more excited about the wedding than even I am. I am really glad because a lot of guys kind of just go through the motions with a wedding, but he isn't one of them. He said that whatever I needed he would help me. Even down to picking the dress. I had to draw the line there. This may be my second wedding, but I am still a traditional girl and want to keep some things that way. I have a whole book of ideas that I can't wait to show you!" I reached over and checked to be sure I'd tossed the my handmade bridal collage in the car.

"That's great he is so on board. I can't believe how he kind of came into your life from nowhere and swept you off your feet like he did. I always knew you would have a romance like it was right off the movie screen. Were you really surprised when he proposed at the Grand Canyon? You had to have had an inkling...come on!" Jill laughed into the phone when I told her I'd had no clue. "Well, he certainly knows what he's doing! I guess you finally found your Cary Grant with the wicked sense of humor."

"That's exactly what I want to capture with the wedding! Hollywood movie magic! My experience working in Hollywood and your artistic eye – we can make it happen!" I was nearly breathless just talking about it.

"Heather, I can hardly think of anything else! We really need to get the venue hammered out. I know we have plenty of white sandy beach here for the ceremony but we gotta have somewhere for the reception. Are you sure you wanna do it barefoot? You know how much we love shoes!"

"Yes, I'm sure. It's what I've always wanted and I can get fabulous shoes for the reception afterward. It's just like you to worry about the shoes." I smiled, Jill was the fashionista and I was the fashionista-in-training, still going to her for advice on clothes and shoes.

She must have been reading my mind. "By the way how are the new shoes and wardrobe we picked out for the job?" she asked. "Everything still going well? You enjoying it?"

"Oh yes! I am really feeling at home there. Thirty employees to oversee is a bit of a process; not to mention the fifty vendors. But you know me, what interest I lack in fashion I make up for with cosmetics, like it's in my blood. The store is beautiful and I feel really good about the difference I can make there. Honestly I couldn't be happier right now."

"You seem to have it all figured out Girly Girl. You deserve it all. I am so happy for you!" Jill's voice kind of cracked as if she might be choking up a little.

"I can't believe we have known each other for ten years. Phew! Through all the marriages, divorces, funerals! Not to forget the fun as well! You are such a dear friend. Thank you for always being there!" Why were we so emotional that morning?

"Aw, thanks Doll. I can't wait to stand up there with you on your special day! You are going to be such a beautiful bride."

"Thanks, sweetie! Okay, I gotta go cause I am pulling up to the store. See you tonight at six." I unhooked my seatbelt and grabbed my purse.

"I'll be there with bells on. Bye!"

"Bye!" I beeped my Jeep locked and headed toward the door. Today was going to be a great day.

Remember that challenges don't come with warning labels. There were no Challenge Ahead road signs to alter my course. No flashing yellow lights to warn me of potential danger ahead. No black cats crossed my path. Just one brown cardboard box left carelessly in a stockroom walkway on the way to my office. Bam! Challenge! I tripped over the box and fell violently forward striking the front of my head, first on a heavy metal shelf, knocking me unconscious, and then again striking my head as I fell face first onto the concrete floor. I lay there unconscious for an unknown length of time.

"Oh my God! Someone call 911!"

"Did anyone see what happened? I was just talking to her a few minutes ago. Is she breathing?"

"I think so, but I don't want to move her. She is out cold."

I was still unconscious and completely unresponsive when the paramedics arrived. A helicopter transported me to a special trauma center an hour away from Sarasota.

When I came to in the trauma center TW was by my side, a beacon of love and light that protected me from panic as I took in the tubes running out of my body, the IV attached to my hand, and the terrible striking pain that permeated my body. My bones ached, even the inside of my nose stung from the strong sterile smell that infected the sheets.

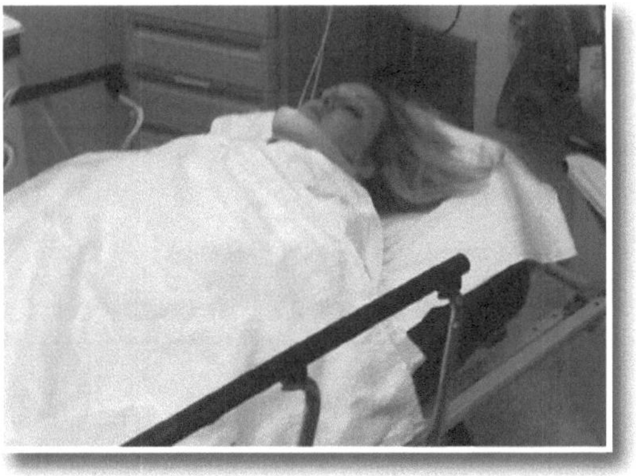

Maybe it was the first night in the trauma center, perhaps the second, I don't know for sure but what I know for certain is that I felt like a frightened child. TW had long been chased from my room with the end of visiting hours and it was just me and those beeping, hissing monitors; sentinels of unknown terror. What would become of me?

I couldn't speak clearly. My legs were frozen in place. And why was the room still spinning?

The questions kept coming: What is really wrong with me? How will this effect my life? How long will this last? How could this happen? Why me? With TW gone, panic hung over me like a filthy, ragged mosquito net that keeps nothing out and only serves to make you hate the place you are in all the more.

I had to get a hold of myself! I *had* to find some way to comfort myself. A deep breath, concentrate...I am in bed – the epitome of a safe place for most of us — so I started with that thought, *I am safe.* I gave myself a hug beneath the rough white blanket. I had the funny thought that what I really wanted was to wrap myself in bubble wrap from my head to my toes. *I am safe.*

The bubble wrap thought became a full-blown image in my mind and I wondered if I were wrapped head-to-toe in bubble wrap would that mean that every time I rolled over I would go pop, pop, pop? That funny and ridiculous notion gave me the sense of comfort I was seeking and I grabbed onto that lifeline. My inward smile, that small slice of humor, gave me hope that I could get myself back on track even in the midst of this uncertainty. But how was I going to do that? Get myself back on track? I couldn't even get to the bathroom on my own!

There are few fans of uncertainty and I am no exception; I had to try and concentrate on what I knew for sure. I wanted more than anything to plan my wedding and get married to TW. I decided to hold on to that vision and block out everything else.

During the months of rehabilitation I had to believe that in every moment of unpredictability, and there were many, that I had the power to choose my future. I had to maintain belief in a good outcome. I had to hold on to the vision of me walking down the aisle and marrying the man I loved.

Fortunately, I was very familiar with Jack Canfield's visualization technique and although I couldn't recall who our president was at the time, I had not forgotten how to visualize a desire, a need, a positive outcome. So I had my big vision; me in a beautiful gown, floating down an aisle to wed my beloved, but I began to feel a bit overwhelmed. How was I going to move forward with a wedding and walk down the aisle in my present helpless and wounded condition? I couldn't even touch my own nose.

Visualization not only aids in manifestation but it also relaxes the body and the mind. Shortly after I began my daily, sometimes hourly visualization exercises, I had the realization that moving forward required a first step. Literally, a step! One foot in front of the other; however, I couldn't yet sit up on my own. Process of elimination guided me to my first plan of action: practice sitting up on my own. I was "lost in space" meaning I had no sense of where my body was in space but I set a goal to do whatever it took to sit up by myself. I felt that I had good support people around me and I knew they would show me the way. When that soft, small voice whispers in your ear and says *I can do this!* your body releases some of it's tension and relaxes a bit; I believe it's possible that our bodies sometimes have belief in positive outcomes even when our mind isn't there yet.

This journey was not a chosen one. I never pointed to a picture of a grayish hospital room with faded bedding and said, "Let's go there!" But, I was going to choose how I was going to travel, one step at a time and then I was going to run!

After my visualization practice was solid and I began making swift headway with sitting up on my own I decided to share the practice with TW. I knew that if I told him about focusing on the big picture and choosing my next steps that he would help keep me on track. He would help me stay focused on my goals especially when the going got tough. I knew there would be times when I would want to quit and I needed to have someone to cheer me on. Mine could not be the *only* hope*ful* heart!

People naturally gravitate towards positive attitudes. We all want to see people be successful no matter what the challenge or goal. I focused on one step at a time while keeping my big goal (my wedding!) in mind. It was kind of like sitting up in bed and fixing your gaze on your finger in front of your eyes. In the distance you see your feet, they are a bit fuzzy but you know that they are there. It's all about perspective. My passion for setting goals (next steps!) and achieving them worked like magic and soon all my friends, family, nurses and doctors were supporting me in my quest to get back on my feet; my enthusiasm for restored health was fueled by hope and faith in a good outcome.

Being full of hope or hope*ful* means believing that no matter where you are in your challenging situation; the beginning, the middle or the end, that you can visualize the outcome as being positive. One of my favorite sayings illustrates this perspective very well: In the end everything will be fine and if it isn't fine, then it isn't the end.

Of course, when you're dead-stuck in the middle of a crisis it can be nearly impossible to summon up hope, but think about this: the crisis you are in now is never your first rodeo. If you take a chaos inventory of your life you can no doubt come up with at least two or three really awful situations that you were able to turn around for the better. No one who has ever had appendicitis has ever wanted his or her appendix back. That is because the challenge of surgery and the recovery progress was just that – progress. In the end you got the outcome you desired which was to feel well again.

What I hope I have shown you here is a way to make the process of recovery easier no matter who you are or what you may be facing. From business challenges to personal crisis's, remaining hope*ful* is the first step on the journey to go from HELPless to HELPful.

Here are your Hope*ful* Steps. Remember: Hope is the starting place for going from Helpless to Helpful! You have the HELPability® to do this...

Write down your current challenge or seemingly hopeless concern or situation:

Write down what you believe to be the best possible outcome from your current challenge or seemingly hopeless concern or situation:

Describe in detail what this best possible outcome will look like:

Describe what the first logical step will be for you to take towards reaching this best possible outcome:

Make a commitment to visualizing this first step and the ultimate BIG PICTURE every day. Write down the time of day you will practice visualization:

Make a list of everyone you can count on to support you in your first step and subsequent steps towards achieving your best possible outcome *(Share your vision with your support team. It has been proven that people who share their goals with others are much more likely to attain their goals.)*:

My first days of working at my new job.

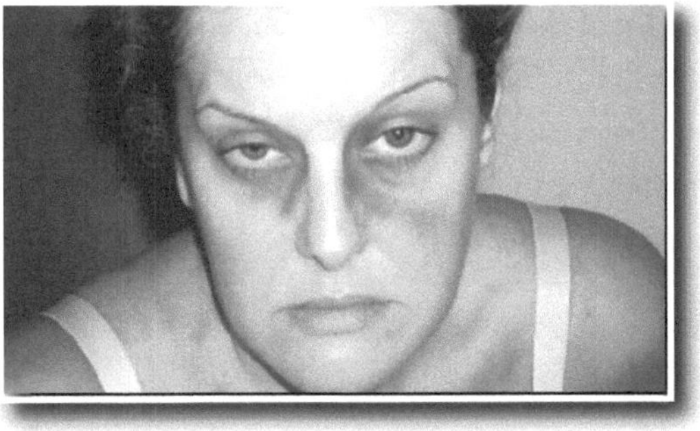

My face as a brain injured person.

CHAPTER THREE

ENCOURAGEMENT

Inspire Others With Courage

"Most of us, swimming against the tides of trouble the world knows nothing about, need only a bit of praise or encouragement and we will make the goal."

—Robert Collier

Heather's Journal Entry: August 25, 2011

"What if I never get any better than I am right now? (That's such a frightening thought!) I can say I am happy to be here, for starters. Actually, I am happy to be ANYWHERE right now. And I know that no matter what happens, I will be the best me I can be and help other people."

What does it mean to feel encouraged? How do you feel when you give encouragement? How do you feel when you are the recipient of encouragement? In my life, encouragement has become the incoming tide that washes my emotional shores clear of all debris; allowing me to swim against the tide despite any fear or trepidation. A clear emotional shoreline clears the way for courage to enter and move us forward towards the horizons of our new days; through the other side of our troubles or challenges. Fear is a very deep and powerful emotion that we all deal with on a daily basis at some level; encouragement from self or others will give us the strength to go the distance required in any given challenge. *I can do this! You can do this!*

Consider examples of encouraging behavior in yourself from past, perhaps lesser trials than you may be facing at this moment. Perhaps you rescued a stray dog from heavy traffic? Others, witnessing this courageous act of kindness may have been encouraged or inspired to do the same the next time they see a frightened dog trying to cross a road on his own. Or, maybe you were the single mother, raising three children on her own that went back to college full-time and got her law degree? Can you imagine how this would be an inspiration to other mothers facing similar circumstances? How they might be able to summon up the courage to *go for it* as you did?

Let us examine the encouraging behaviors of others that have inspired us to action. Maybe someone who inspires you is close to home; a neighbor, who serves our country in Afghanistan and leaves his beloved family for months at a time to fight in dangerous, god-forsaken war zones. Or, how about your dearest friend with small children and a full-time job that stills find the time to volunteer at the senior center every Tuesday night. And who among us does not have at least one member of our family or extended family who, despite battling a chronic or terminal illness, still manages to go to the playground with their children or grandchildren and wouldn't think about missing one of their soccer games?

If we fully examine all examples of encouraging behavior we will find that at the core of the courageous act is selflessness. We don't worry we might get hurt as we attempt to save the dog in traffic. We summon the physical and mental strength to study for a college course at 10 o'clock in the evening despite having worked all-day and cared for our children. We push through the pain and debilitation of MS, grab our walker or our crutches and we get our butts to that soccer game and cheer our grandchild on!

Has there been a time in your life that someone really needed you but you might not have been doing so hot at the time yourself? However, you got out of your own head, followed your heart and showed them your courage and were able to offer them the support that they required?

And conversely, can you recall a time when you ignored your inner knowing and failed to act on your inspiration to assist? Without judgement, examine how you felt about the two different scenarios. One, where you exhibited encouraging behavior; and the other when you didn't or felt that you couldn't?

Is it possible that the encouraging behavior(s) left you feeling help*ful*? Are you open to the possibility that inaction resulted in your feeling help*less*? This is why ENCOURAGEMENT is the next stage of going from HELPless to HELPful and how it can enable you to move through your personal challenges in business and life more easily.

Let me share with you how, after about three weeks into my rehabilitation I learned the valuable lesson of the power of ENCOURAGEMENT in my own life and how it taught me to be HELPful no matter my limitations and how to inspire others with my courage.

TW glanced up from his laptop to peer out the window, "Looks like it is going to be coming down all day." Rain slammed against the window so hard it looked like we were in a giant car wash.

"Yeah, weird for Florida. Reminds me more of Michigan." I snuggled lower into my bed, pressed the button to lower my pillow.

"I hear ya." TW closed his laptop and came over and sat on the edge of the bed. His smile was all the sunshine I needed.

"Ya know, you don't have to stay all day again today. I'll be fine." I pushed him on the leg, "Go, go home and get some real rest! It's Sunday so I won't have physical therapy and I kinda wanna just bunker in and sleep."

He laughed, "You're not getting rid of me! I have been here every day from first thing in the morning til I tuck you in at night and I am not changing that today."

Despite my current less than desirable physical and mental state, I felt like the luckiest girl in the world to have this man love me. "Thank you, Babe. That means so much to me. You've been my rock through this."

He kissed me on the forehead, "I wouldn't have it any other way. I love you! Now, let's see if we can find a movie on tv."

"Uhm, okay...but it's hard for me to watch for long. The movements and the flickering of the lights...I can always look away when I need to and just listen."

"I'd really love to share our movie time again. Just try? For me? Okay?"

He looked so happy at the possibility of doing something so seemingly small yet so wonderfully enjoyable and *normal* for us. I knew I had to try, but...

"It's also important that you try to stay awake as much as possible today." TW reminded me. "I know your brain just wants to sleep but the doctor says you need to try and stay awake and stimulate your brain as much as possible."

"Babe, I just get so tired so quickly. Like, I could sleep right now."

"I know, Sweet Pea but let's see what we can find. Maybe not a whole movie, just a show? How about that?" He clicked through the channels. "I'm a little hungry. How about you?"

I knew what he wanted. Our Super Snack-Bearing-Fairy Godmother, Magda my caregiver who would arrive with her pockets full of graham crackers, peanut butter and tiny milk cartons like the ones we used to get in grade school. She was the embodiment of comfort. Funny how something as simple as peanut butter and graham crackers could bring so much peace in the midst of chaos.

I smiled back at TW and said, "Sure, I could use a snack. Let's see if Magda is here today."

"Well, push that Fairy Godmother button and let's see if she appears."

"I'm on it." The buzzer was precariously perched on the nightstand a bit too far for me to easily reach. My initial instinct was to ask TW to hand it to me. Then my better-than-initial-instinct spoke up and shouted *do it yourself! You can do it!* And so I pressed the button to raise my bed, used my arms to re-position my butt nearer to the edge of the mattress, pulled my lifeless legs to the side, braced myself with one hand against the bed-railing and grabbed onto the buzzer all by myself. Tiny steps forward!

"Oh Babe, It's *I Love Lucy*, your favorite! A marathon, no way!"

"Oh my gosh! It's perfect." I loved Lucy. Right away I recognized the episode. "I love this one. It's the one where she stomps the wine."

"Look at her face!" TW adored Lucy almost as much as I did.

"Hey Magda!"

"Hullo there! You two ready for your favorite snack?" She smiled her big broad smile; her hands digging around her enormous pockets for our goodies.

"You betchya!" TW pushed the tray cart over towards Magda so she could unload her treasures.

"Thank you so much!"

"You need anything, just anything you call Magda huh?"

"Ok, we will and thank you!"

"Let's get the buffet rollin!" TW reached for the milk I was about to open. "Let me open your milk for you, you know how messy you get." He laughed.

I feigned horror, "I do not!"

"And don't try to pawn this off on your brain, you were way messy before that happened."

"I so was not!"

"Were too!" He playfully poked my arm, "Messy! Messy! Messy!"

I ignored his antics because something on the television screen had grabbed my attention. It was a restored memory! "Oh wow, this is my absolute favorite one. The Vita one! I remember it so well! I love this episode!"

"The what?" TW asked.

"The one where she is drinking the vitamin stuff in the commercial and gets drunk. Vitamedia somthing. Do you pop out at parties? Are you unpoopular?" I was actually laughing.

"Oh yeah. Cool!" TW was laughing with me now, "I do remember this one!"

This was the first time we had shared a genuine laugh since my fall. Sometimes it is the teeniest, tiny things...

TW just stared at me with a look of peace I had not seen in weeks. He smiled as he told me, "Wow! This is the first time I have seen you laugh like that in so long."

"My head hurts a little but it was worth it. It felt really, really good!"

"Seeing you like that just made my heart smile. We are going to be okay, ya know?"

"Yes, I do now. Everything is going to be okay." And I believed that.

TW's cartoons that he drew on the board of my hospital room to make me laugh.

TW and I had witnessed first hand what Norman Cousins had discovered, that laughter indeed was the best medicine and has healing power. We were both feeling the effects of fear of the unknown. We had no idea what the future held with my recovery and what our lives would look like in the coming months.TW and I needed to encourage each other during this crucial time. Even though it was difficult for me to watch TV and push my limits in that way, I knew I needed to do what I could to encourage my fiancée. Many times in the face of chaos it is the simplest acts of normalcy that can restore order as well as confidence, which in turn inspires courage in any given situation.

Although you may not think that simply watching an episode of *I Love Lucy* displayed courage; considering the fragile nature of the brain that has been traumatized; the simple act of watching television could have triggered over-sensitizing my brain resulting in a massive, highly painful migraine, or cause my body to begin to tremble and shake in a defensive reaction.

Intuitively, I knew we needed to experience something normal from our life prior the accident. My inner voice guided me to take a risk to gain a sense of peace and order; not only for me but for TW who had thought he was getting a successful, strong independent woman as his future wife. Instead, the possibility of being caregiver to a newly dependent, mentally and physically impaired wife loomed darkly on his horizon. That spontaneous shared laughter over that *Lucy* episode was the single most important moment in my recovery up to that time. We needed that peace to wash over us like a cool breeze on a hot day. All that matters in those precious moments of victory is that you receive a sense that things will be ok again.

I felt a real sense that I was returning to myself and that my inner strength was flexing it's muscles displaying courage. The visualizations were an every day practice, my personal-test taking (getting the buzzer from the nightstand on my own!), laughter returned and I could see a change on TW's face which in turn inspired me to do more; to push harder still. TW was good at putting on a smile and was quick with a joke but I saw the slightest easing in his face and the tension in his eyes dissipate a little after our shared laughter. Even with all my symptoms raging on and confined to a wheelchair I had been able to display courage and encourage the most important person in my life.

Do you need encouragement in your life at this time? Are there people in your life that need encouragement? How will you muster up your courage to be that living example for someone who needs it? Remember: Giving encouragement to yourself and to others who are facing challenges is giving the gift of inspiration. When we are encouraged, we inspire others with our living example!

Here are your Encouragement Steps. Encouragement is the second step for going from Helpless to Helpful!

Acknowledge the courage you have inside. What was the last thing you did that was courageous and how do you think it may have encouraged or inspired others? Write a short synopsis here:

What are you afraid of? The father of the modern success movement, Napoleon Hill, studied fear and actually named and described all the fears we face. Recognizing your fears may be the most beneficial way to build your courage so that you can be encouraging. List your top fears here:

Despite your current challenge(s) what are some ways you can be a living example of courage for others? Write three possibilities here:

Select a favorite inspiring or encouraging quote and memorize it. Repeat this quote throughout the day; allow it to become your mantra and share it with others. Write it down here:

TW and I laughing and being silly in the days before my accident.
Good practice to face what was to come later.

CHAPTER FOUR

LOVE

Passionate Affection

"Forgiving the past means remembering the love there and releasing the rest as the illusion that it really was."
—Marianne Williamson

Heather's Journal Entry: September 23, 2013

"I can hardly believe the events of the past few weeks. How am I supposed to make sense of all this? Right now I can't. What I can do is remember that no matter how many times I get knocked down, the next thing to do is get up"

Tender. Warm. Affectionate regard. Friendship. Admiration. Compatibility. Warm personal attachment. Fondness. Benevolence. Passionate affection. All words and phrases used to define the word *love* by Webster's Dictionary.

Hate. Dislike. Aversion. Scorn. Contempt. Malice. Ill will. Bitterness. Antipathy. Detestation. Loathing. Animosity. All words and phrases used to define the antithesis of *love.*

Why then, is it so difficult for so many of us to ask for help from the people that we love and who love us? Read those words! We should be drawn to the people in our lives who love us like bees to honey. Why do many of us feel it is wrong to ask for help or reassurance from our most solid supporters? Are we confused about the nature of our most intimate relationships? Are we afraid that we will appear weak in the eyes of people who care for us? Are we afraid others will view us as incapable? Do we lose face when we ask for help? Do we gain face by suffering alone?

When was the last time you heard the phrase *you have got to pull yourself up by your bootstraps*? Many of us may have heard it from our parents; or, depending on your age, your hard-scrabble grandparents who may have lived through the Great Depression or the lesser known Toilet Paper Shortage and Gas Shortages of the mid 1970s. This saying highlights a common thread of behavior that is prevalent throughout our culture, you have to go it alone and you must conquer your challenges by yourself or die trying. Furthermore, if you're a woman, you'd better look pretty while you're doing it.

I believe that self-control and willpower are important skills that have endless merit, and when applied appropriately can be important assets to living a full and successful life. However, they are not the be all and end all life tenets when it comes to overcoming a challenge.

Most of us have heard many inspirational speakers talk about the power of taking personal responsibility. My view has a bit of a twist to that concept. I believe it is the height of personal responsibility to get your eyes off of yourself and help someone else. In my experience "bootstrapping" causes a tremendous amount of unnecessary emotional and mental strain not to mention possible lengthy delays in achieving the best possible outcome in many situations. Of course, if you're drowning I'm not suggesting you don't focus on yourself and start treading water like your life depended on it – because it does!

What I'm suggesting is that to ask for help *is to help*; to *not ask* for help blocks out any possibility for you to experience love from another. We deny others opportunities to extend a hand and it leaves us each alone and focused on our own troubles until we become our troubles; our illness, or our situation. We are no longer Heather O'Brien Walker but instead people know us as Brain Trauma Girl! Or, there goes Whiplash Woman! Hey there! Yeah, you, Methamphetamine Man! Foreclosure Frank! Get the picture?

It is a solid truth that people would rather avoid pain than seek pleasure, so why are we deliberately causing ourselves pain by refusing to ask for help? How was I able to recognize that I was actually causing myself more pain during my healing process? Because I was one of the worst offenders of bootstrapping!

Over the years I had developed into the type who thought no one could do it better than me, I didn't need anyone. I prided myself on the fact that my employees, family and friends looked up to me for facing challenges all by myself, with little help from anyone.

This adaptive behavior was not a trait I was born with. As a child I asked for help with my math homework and I certainly didn't teach myself to drive a car. But, when I was a young adult, like many of you, I had been let down by someone who I trusted and relied on. My first husband had vowed to always be there for me and he didn't keep that vow. In fact, to say he didn't keep that vow is putting it kindly. Nevertheless, he taught me what felt like for many years an invaluable lesson: Never let that happen again. Depend on no one except myself. Don't ever ask for help again.

Have you ever made a promise like that to yourself thinking it would keep you from ever experiencing pain or disappointment again? That *Lone Ranger* way of thinking served me well for only so long. It certainly didn't serve me as I was recovering from my second brain injury, that was a result of a car accident on my way home from a doctor appointment for ongoing treatment for the first brain injury.

I had only recently been released from the rehabilitation hospital. TW had thorough instructions as to how to best care for me at home. TW took me to work with different therapists during the day to assist with my exercises but for the most part, TW was the nurse on call 24/7. It was during this time that I learned the power of releasing oneself to the fact that others want to show their love by reaching out with passionate affectionate during our most dire circumstances.

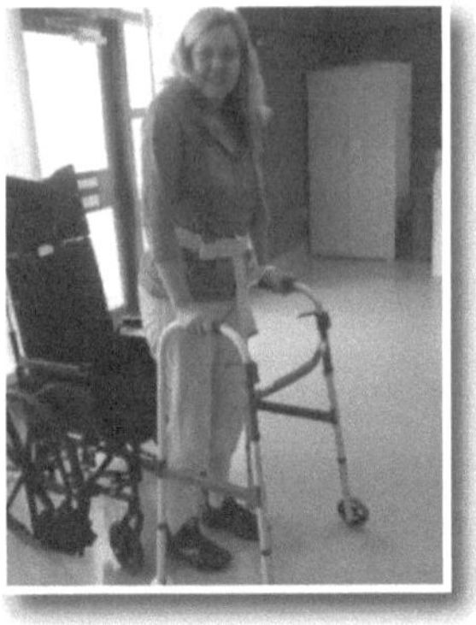

Standing on my own for the first time. Notice the special high backed wheelchair that helps to keep me from falling out of my chair due to disorientation.

Evening was rolling into full-blown night and it was time to begin thinking about going to bed. Pre-multiple-brain-trauma-life didn't require *thinking about* going to bed. TW and I would just go to bed. Now there was a wheelchair to commandeer to the bathroom. I had to be lifted out of it, onto the toilet, into the shower or the tub. What face cleanser did I need? Did my legs need shaved? Or, who the hell cares?

TW rolled me into the bedroom towards the bathroom. "Let's get started with your shower young lady."

"No! No shower! It hurts my skin too much. I just can't take it tonight. It's been a rough day."

"Are you sure? I'll get in there with you. Shave your legs for you?"

"No, Babe. I really appreciate it. But, the water hitting my skin is too painful. I know it's weird."

"No, I get it. The brain is a complicated; it gets bashed around, it spits out weirdness."

"Yeah, I guess so. I just wish it would hurry up and heal."

"You are doing remarkable young lady and I don't want to

hear anything else but that come out of your mouth. So, a bath it is!"

TW lifts me out of the wheelchair and gently lowers me into the tub. I sink into the bubble bath; it feels like a warm hug easing my whole body into complete relaxation.

"The water is perfect. Thank you so much; for the lift and running it for me."

"I'll let you be. Call me if you need anything and when you're ready to get out."

"Okay. I'm good for now."

After a nice, long soak, bliss interrupted my negative-think and ruminations about my current condition and gave way to a realization: steeped in self-pity as I was at that moment, I decided to take my eyes off myself and give TW a break. So, I grabbed ahold of the side of the tub, braced myself with what I thought was a good grip and foisted myself up and slipped over the edge – right onto the wet tile floor! Thankfully, I did not hit my head but the fall shook me up enough to bring tears to my eyes. Lying there like a wet towel; I called out for TW. The tile was so cold, I was wet and in such pain; waves of anger and defeat washed over me even as TW lifted me into his arms. That was it – I was giving up. I thought for certain that if you Googled "giving up" you'd find my pathetic picture. I pushed away from TW's arms.

"Are you ok? What happened?" TW's face said it all; he was horrified and frightened.

"I wanted to give you a break so I tried to get out on my own. I thought I could make it to the chair." Pain came in waves; I could feel a spasm coming on.

"You're all wet. You look like a pile of dirty laundry." He laughed; his attempt to bring humor into the scary situation.

"I give up!" I sobbed, "I can't do this anymore! I just can't handle it!"

"Babe, let me help you. Let's get you dry. You'll feel better." TW reached for a dry towel. "Here, let me help you."

"Put me down! Just leave me alone!" Frustration and raw emotion fueled my rage. I felt so helpless!

"Why are you doing this? Let me help you." TW was insistent.

"No! Get away from me – just leave me here!"

"Don't you understand," he said, "when you hurt, I hurt and when you feel good I feel good."

"Really?"

"Yes, really. And I want to talk to you about something." He wrapped me up in a fluffy towel and made sure I was comfortable in my chair. "Comfy?"

"Yes. What is it you want to talk about?"

TW knelt down in front of me, took a hold of both arms of the wheelchair and looked into my eyes as he said, "I think we need to set the date."

"What date?" Then I knew! "What? After what just happened? You must be joking!"

"I am very serious."

I was livid. "Absolutely not! I have been through ENOUGH! The fall, the car accident! I'm in no shape for a wedding. The planning, the work, the stress…I can't do it."

Stupid visualizations! How naïve I had been! This wedding is never going to happen. The negative thoughts rammed my battered brain one after the other as I sat there in my wheelchair, trapped.

TW went on, "I think it's important."

"I certainly don't picture me on my wedding day rolling down the aisle in this thing, embarrassing myself. I'm still slurring my words. The whole idea sounds like a nightmare. Forget what I said about my visualizations – forget I ever mentioned my picture of the beautiful, ideal wedding. IT'S NEVER GOING TO HAPPEN! Look at me! Do you want to be saddled with this? This could be as good as it gets!"

"You don't understand."

"No, YOU don't understand! I want to marry you but not like this. I want it to be the picture! The perfect movie I've spent hours focusing on in my messed up brain."

"I do understand that. But I still want to set the date."

"Now, I don't understand." Was this man crazy?

"You are going to become Mrs. TW Walker, so I think it's really important for you to *walk* down the aisle. We need to set the date and that becomes our goal; for you to walk down the aisle on your own. I know you can do it. You've spent weeks on this visualization – you believe in that power. I know you do."

I looked at him a good long while before I responded, "I do believe it." I couldn't resist him anymore. "You're right. I do believe it."

"You have to believe it, for no other reason than I'm not changing my name to TW Wheelchair!"

We laughed. The wet tub — that anyone could have slipped on — was not going to win this one. TW took my hand and brought it to his lips and kissed it. He had been doing that for me since our very first date. It was a very special moment of passionate affection exchanged between us in the midst of challenge.

In those moments on the wet, cold bathroom floor, I learned that allowing someone to help you is not about you being help*less*, it's about you being help*ful*. We can bring opportunity to others to be HELPful, when we allow them to support us. I can't think of a higher form of service to another or a more loving thing to do for someone.

Recall the most recent situation in which you helped someone. Did you feel the love coming from inside of you? When you feel that warm and sunny feeling welling up in you there is no longer room for fear and anxiety. It frees you up to have power over your own current trial or challenge. Also, when you let someone help you, you open yourself up to receive love from another person allowing you to again ease your fear and anxiety. Love going out, love coming in; like the tide.

Once again I realized that this path towards recovery wasn't all about me. TW's life was impacted greatly by my struggles as well as his own recovery from subsequent back and foot surgeries following our car accident. Scan your life and examine how your challenge may be affecting the people around you? Are you shutting out their help? Are you closing yourself off to the love and support that could actually make this challenge easier on you and them? The hand I had been dealt was TW's hand to play as well. I wasn't in the game alone. By allowing him to give and serve me I opened his wellspring of passionate affection towards me. Truth is, no one overcomes and perseveres, succeeds or achieves without the HELPfulness of others.

Here are your Love steps. Remember: Love is the third step for moving forward from Helpless to Helpful!

Take an inventory of all the love (passionate affection) you have in your life and write down the names of all your passionate affection givers:

Recall how you felt the most recent time you received passionate affection and list the feelings here:

Watch for love from strangers. Remember love comes in many, many forms. I recall a day that I was lost on a city street and a gentleman came out of a restaurant and asked how he could help me. He knew just where I needed to go... Note a time when you received love from a stranger or gave love to a stranger:

How difficult is it for you to ask for help? Investigate how comfortable you are with receiving help; are there rules you have created in your mind about why it is not okay to ask? If so, right those rules down on a separate piece of paper. Go crazy with it! Write them all down – THEN TEAR IT UP AND THROW IT AWAY!!!

What opportunities do you have to display your love to others? List 3 opportunities and the date by which you expect to accomplish your goal of giving love (or passionate affection) to someone in need here:

A challenging outing to the beach for me. Some days TW had to pry me out of the house for my own good. Getting a cuddle from our dog Jack always helped me.

CHAPTER FIVE

POSITIVITY

Moving In A Beneficial Direction

"If one advances confidently in the direction of his dreams, and endeavors to live the life which he has imagined, he will meet with a success unexpected in common hours."
—Henry David Thoreau

Heather's Journal Entry: January 13, 2013

"I don't know why some people seem to have more to deal with than others. What I do know is that I am not going to waste my energy focusing on all that may be considered "wrong" with me. I choose to focus on all the things that are "right" with me and my ability to move in the direction of my dreams no matter how small that step may be."

When you hear the word positivity, what comes to mind? A Cheerleader Personality who jumps on every word you utter reminding you to not be so negative and instead turn your frown upside down? Although that is an amusing image, that is not the path of positivity that I want to talk with you about here.

When I talk about positivity I am referring to the act of moving forward in a beneficial direction; even if the only thing you can muster is one small step. We all know from experience that the first step is always the hardest. But guess what? As with any behavior, the more we practice the easier the behavior becomes. And, when applied to dealing with crisis or challenges in our lives, the easier it becomes to live in the here and now, leaving that last challenge behind in the dust; a memory we can call on only when needed to assist us in a current journey through challenge.

Think back to your most recent triumph over challenge. What did it feel like to take those small steps in the beginning? Do you recall how awesome each step felt as you moved closer to the other side of your challenge? Perhaps you found a new job after a sudden layoff; your weeks of pounding the pavement and networking within your field finally paid off. Or, did the bank threaten to foreclose on your home but through your patient negotiation agreed to refinance your house instead of taking it from you. Then there are the physical challenges that not only can zap our emotional and physical strength, but our finances and our interpersonal relationships as well. However, despite the odds, you were able to step through the darkest of days out into a sunnier world on the other side of your particular life occurrence.

If this book has found you once again in the beginning or middle of a new catastrophe or challenge; take a moment right now to breath in the light of success that you experienced after the last challenge was all said and done. You can feel that way again, I promise you. You just have to begin right now. Once again, set a goal for success or better yet make a promise to yourself. Making a promise adds emotional intensity to your goal. Any movement in the direction of your goal will create the momentum that can carry you through the darkest nights of your challenge(s) and out the other side. Be aware that it is crucial to celebrate even the smallest victories as you begin to move forward.

Like a train beginning to pull a load down the track, the wheels slip and spin a bit and the engine huff and puffs but eventually the wheels gain traction and the entire train begins the journey. I was certainly doing my share of huffing and puffing as TW and I did our "wedding walk" practice three times a day. It was one thing to walk on a hard flat surface but to walk in sand is completely different. Walking through sand ups the ante tenfold under any circumstances. For someone who wobbles like a Weeble on smooth pavement, sand is a No Mans Land. Only one thing eased my mind during those practice walks: if I tripped and fell at least I would have a soft landing.

•••

"Come on, let's get the lead out!" Barking like a drill sergeant was TW's way of *inspiring* me to march down the short road to the beach.

"Very funny, Sergeant!"

"That's right, forward march!"

"You sound just like David. You know he is former military right? When I am really moaning and groaning during therapy he'll say 'No no, the only acceptable response is thank you sir, may I have another?' like in *Animal House*."

TW laughed. "Ha! I knew I liked that guy."

"Yeah, two peas in a pod. Anita has the exact opposite approach. She's very tender. And intuitive. She knows what's going on with me before I can tell her. Good thing, too, since in the beginning all I could do was basically gurgle and mumble."

"She is a real sweetheart for sure."

"They both have completely different approaches but I owe them so much for their dedication and care. I would never be able to do this without their help."

"That's for sure." TW looked out across the beach, "Well, here we are. Let's do this!"

"Okay, here I go." I stepped onto the sand. The warmth began to relax my body immediately. "Keep talking so I can distract my mind a bit; otherwise my warning bells will sound and I will get too scared to move."

TW moved closer, "Do you want my arm?"

"Maybe, to get me started. Gosh, the beach is different each day, new bumps and ridges from the wind and tide. I get a new obstacle course everyday."

"Very true. You're doing great by the way." TW patted my hand on his arm, "So how is your dress coming?"

"Ah, you certainly know how to distract me. I am so excited about it! I am so glad I am having it made and it's going to be so unique. I don't know if I ever told you why I decided this was for sure the ONE."

"Even if you have, tell me again."

"I knew since I first saw *The Secret* and learned from Jack Canfield about visualizing that I had to visualize myself walking down an aisle. You know, I've been doing that visualization since back in rehab. Then, when we set the date I had to alter the visualization to include me in my special dress."

The more excited I became with my explanation, the smoother my steps in the sand. "Anyhow, I had to figure out a way to feel beautiful while living in the wheelchair and not being able to walk. I thought, what is beautiful but can't walk? Then it hit me! A mermaid!"

"Oh wow. That's really cool."

"Yeah, right? So, when I saw the dress that had the hand painted mermaids on it, I knew it was the one. Now my visualization is me as a mermaid that has just emerged from the ocean dripping with starfish and is feeling the soft sand between her toes and begins her first walk on the beach."

"I am so proud of you. It's going to be amazing. I can't wait to see you walk down that aisle in that dress on our wedding day."

"I'm so excited! Helen, the artist, is customizing everything for me, so it will be the only dress of it's kind. It's going to be perfect, just like we planned." My steps were solid, longer. My legs felt strong and fully able to support me as we strolled along the beach.

TW stopped in his tracks, taking my face into his hands, he looked me in the eyes and said, "Hey, I believe it! I believe in you!"

"Thank you, Babe. Your support means everything." I gave him a big hug. "Now, how about we head back to the house; I've got an appetite worked up."

"Your wish is my command, young lady."

"I want to try some alone walking so you go ahead and I will follow you okay?"

"You sure?"

"Yes, I'm good. Keep talking to me though."

"Okay. So, you and Jill are still working on the starfish centerpieces with the stones right?"

"Yes, sir, we are."

"Great. I can knock out some more fans and bubbles later. Check those off the list. We are rockin' and rollin' don't you think? Babe? Heather?"

"Yes?" I called meekly from my as yet undisclosed location.

"What are you doing over there in the bushes?"

"Um, I don't really know. Help?"

"I gotchya, don't worry."

TW found me floundering around in the huge hedge that lined our street.

"Well that was interesting! I wasn't even aware I was veering off like that. Guess I still have some work to do."

"Ha!" TW laughed, "I am going to have to get you a clapper to wear around your neck so I can keep track of you."

"Weekends only and no way I'm wearing it with my mermaid dress!"

"In all seriousness, Sweet Pea, you have come so far. Don't let this little side trip get you down for even a second. Remember when you first got to the hospital and couldn't sit up on the edge of the bed or even touch your nose?"

"Yes, I do."

"The progress you have made is incredible! We have to always focus on how far you have come." He smiled. "You know, many of the doctors thought you'd never be able to walk on your own."

"You are right. We have to celebrate all the wins, no matter how small."

"Little steps everyday."

"Sometimes I get discouraged when I seem to take what feels like steps back. I guess healing doesn't happen in a straight line. I have to look at it as taking steps to the hedge and not backward."

"Ha! Ha! Exactly! Now let's go celebrate with some lunch."

I won't tell you taking steps forward was easy, because it wasn't. Mastering my balance, stretching sore and battered muscles and trying desperately to lift my legs and move them forward were no small feats. Whether you are facing a physical challenge, an emotional or mental challenge, you still have to find ways to move through it. What are your options really? My only alternative to moving forward was to stay wheelchair bound and dependent on others for all my care. That life was not an option for me, that's where I drew the line. It would have kept not only me bound and stuck, but TW as well.

Is your line in the sand not moving in with your mother because you lost your home? Is it finally acknowledging that you are on the verge of keeling over from a heart attack because you won't get a grip on your eating habits? Your wife and children facing a life without you? Is it not going back to work for someone after your own business fails and refusing to have your life dictated by someone else?

Of course, there are situations where physical injury or illness results in permanent ties to a wheelchair or even a bed. In these cases, it is helpful to ask yourself *what are your options* in dealing with your challenge? Where do you draw your line in the sand as to what is acceptable or unacceptable for you despite insurmountable limitations? You may not have your legs but you have your mind. You may not have your arms but you have your heart. You may not have a year but you have months. Examine your circumstances and reach for the first even tiniest goal. Prisoners of war have often written about finding just one small treasure; seeing a butterfly during the day carried them through what they thought were their final hours. Find joy in the smallest breeze, the slightest smile, the softest sheets, and the sweetest fruit.

I did what I had to do to get out of my wheelchair by helping others to take positive steps with me. I didn't want to just get by and come out of this challenge just okay. I wanted to realize my dream wedding and have TW get back to being focused on his own life, rather than on solely caring for me. It was important for me to look beyond just walking down the aisle. The forward steps I took were just as much, if not more, for TW than for me. If you remember, it was his idea to set the wedding date and have me walk down the aisle on my own. So in working so hard to be able to walk again, I was actually moving in a beneficial direction and helping TW to move forward as well.

Again, our challenges never happen in a vacuum. You have to find the positive steps that help the people around you. More often than not your challenge has taken some of the people in your life off of the track they were on. It certainly did in my case. I was very blessed that my friends and family were concerned about nothing else more than my well being and did whatever they could do to support me. I had to make sure I was always in a place to be grateful to others and receive support from them. I knew it would ease their concern and help them take steps to get them back on their own track. Everyone has their own particular way of expressing love and concern. Many sent beautiful flowers and thoughtful cards. Some came by to visit and would just sit with me; comfortable in the silence. I was gifted with everything from healing prayers to a cozy Winnie-The-Pooh blanket, to warm and comforting macaroni and cheese. It really seemed my phone never stopped ringing and to talk to my family so far away, even for the brief moment I was able to speak was like a lifeline to me. Remember: find joy in the slightest breeze and the smallest gesture to move you forward.

And when the time comes for the people who supported you, as I said before – everyone's time comes - find out what your supporters need to progress in their forward motion and take action to assist them in moving in their beneficial direction. Exude an air of positivity; be a living example of forward motion, like that train rolling down the track.

One of the positive things about any challenge is that it also forces you to rebuild. We all know that for example when we get a new computer or phone, most of us don't mess with the settings. For the most part we leave all the default settings because we want to get rolling as soon as possible. It's only when something goes wrong that we go into screens we never even knew existed and begin to look at all the options there are to choose from. Then we see we can better customize our options so that our computer better reflects our own unique preferences and is more beneficial for us.

Our challenges can be dealt with in the same manner. I am not saying it is easy to do this, especially when the challenge initially clocks you. Being totally transparent with you, there were more times than I care to mention that I felt totally helpless and was sure I was being punished for something I wasn't aware I had done. Finally, after much reflection and developing my HELP philosophy®, which got my eyes off myself, I saw what was happening to me as an opportunity to hit the restart button, reboot my life and make a difference in other people's lives as well.

In all honesty, my life looks completely different than it did prior to the accident. My new perspective is much fuller than it was before, as is TW's. This new view has made me a better person, wife, friend, author, speaker and assures me that my life has purpose and that I can accomplish all that I set out to do. How can your challenge enrich your life? You have the opportunity to reboot. Who do you want to become?

Here are your Positivity steps. Remember: Positivity is the final step for moving forward from Helpless to Helpful!

Who in your life seems to be stuck and could use support in moving forward in a beneficial direction? Write their name(s) here:

What are some steps you have used in your own struggles that you could share with them? Write down the three most important steps you can recall:

Recognize the forward motion of others and how far they have come. Write down the names of three people in your life who have overcome challenge:

Contact each of these three important people and acknowledge their progress and invite them to celebrate their success. It will mean so much that you noticed and help them to feel motivated to keep going in that positive direction. Write down three ways you can help celebrate with these folks (Lunch? Invite them over for coffee? Bake them a cake?) and do it!

Spreading laughter is the key to moving forward in the right direction. Sense of humor is a very personal thing. Find what really tickles someone's funny bone and help them move forward!

Becoming a mermaid at my wedding dress fitting.

CHAPTER SIX

THE HELP MISSION

How You And I Can Make A Difference Together

"Don't give up. Don't lose hope."
Christopher Reeve

Heather's Journal Entry: April 12, 2013

"I found that during my healing journey it was way easier to receive HELP (hope, encouragement, love, positivity) from others when I was in my wheelchair. It was as if there was a neon sign that flashed brightly to everyone that I was working through challenges. Now free of the wheelchair, I still have many challenges, but looking at me no one would know it. I have come to realize that we need to treat others as if everyone is wearing a HELP WANTED sign around their necks."

When I was in the midst of recovery from my first TBI (Traumatic Brain Injury) and then only forty days later experienced a car accident that resulted in a second TBI, I thought I couldn't find the strength to go back to the beginning of another healing challenge. I was overwhelmed with anger, frustration, grief and core-shaking fear. You may have felt similar feelings of desperation so pervasive that your weary head falls into your sweaty palms and it feels as though the air has been knocked out of your lungs. You are dead stuck in the middle of one challenge and don't look now, but another one comes barreling around the corner knocking you another three feet back. We know it happens because the old saying, "when it rains, it pours" is still around today.

This is the real world we are dealing with here and like it or not it is full of challenges. If you are waiting around for that to change, you are going to have a long wait my friend. What we can do, is prepare ourselves to respond to those challenges in a way that ensures our growth and that has the added benefit of helping others. That's what the HELP mission is all about. It's about moving from a place of Helplessness to a place of Helpfulness so that we can effectively and swiftly deal with our challenges with less pain.

You have read my story and I have shared the lessons I learned along the way. I don't think you could argue the fact that I was certainly someone who experienced feeling helpless and at times exhibited symptoms of the deadly victim mentality dis-ease; a very tricky dis-ease if you wish to accomplish much of anything in your life.

Feeling helpless left me physically sick; exhausted; wounded and the worst part? Lonely. I had truly hit bottom. The more tragic result was that I was dragging everyone around me down into the pit of Victim Hell with me. Hell is only one letter off from HELP. I'd like to buy a consonant please? P! Give me another P, *please*! It only takes a small adjustment of one letter to get you moving toward HELPful. I was actually harming the people closest to me. Something I never thought I was capable of doing.

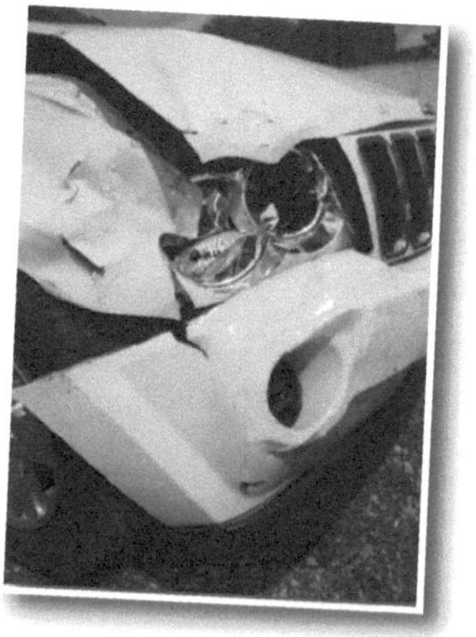

You may ask, is it a difficult task to move from feeling HELPless to HELPful? I'll be honest, yes, maybe; sometimes. However, the truth is, it's doable. In our day of text messaging to anyone, anywhere, anytime and Internet shopping from our easy chairs; any manner of immediate gratification available to us in sometimes only seconds, the self-guided old-school journey to HELPful may seem to some like a long road. But, let's put it in perspective; do you want to live your life tied to the short-lived fire of instant gratification or do you want to live a life buoyed by self-activation and inner strength that can save you in any storm?

Do a self check right now. Stop and ask how am I really feeling? HELPless? Next, evaluate your circumstances and then ask: How can I be Helpful today? It is then that you'll notice the movement of energy around you. We're all comprised of energy, and when we come from a place of HELPfulness the energy gets stronger and even more magnetic; drawing like-minded energy towards you, which in turn provides the clarity and momentum you'll need to move forward into your life and through your challenge.

When I teach breakout sessions at events or workshops, and also when I work with my coaching clients I explain the HELP philosophy®. I then pair people up and ask them to share with their partner a particular challenge they are facing. After they have both had a few minutes to share their challenge, they break. I ask which one of the pair wants to go first with the rest of the exercise. The one who decides to go first, I call the HELPer. I ask the HELPer to trust their instincts that they are capable of helping their partner with their challenge. The HELPer has a few minutes to focus on their partner and give them any manner of hope, encouragement, love and positivity. Human behavior studies tell us that the HELPeris expecting his partner to do the same in return. However, I don't have them go there. I ask the HELPer to reflect back on his/her own challenge as he presented it to his/her partner. I ask the HELPer to examine his/her words of HELP to his/her partner to see if there is something there for himself/herself. Is there something new he never thought of or has he been reminded of something he had forgotten and can now use to help himself/herself? Remember, when we fill a hole in others, we fill a hole in ourselves. I have yet to find a case where the HELPer isn't helped with his/her own challenge, by first giving help to another.

In a recent study published by the Journal of Clinical Oncology, researchers stated that married people with cancer were 20% less likely to die from their disease, compared to people who had no social support. What the researchers concluded from this is that people who have a strong support system boosted their odds of sticking with treatment by 70%! P aul Nguyen, a radiation oncologist at Dana Farber Cancer Institute in Brigham and Women's Hospital in Boston states, "Improving social support for our patients may be equally important as providing effective therapy, and it is less costly to develop and implement." Ayal Aizer, chief resident of the Harvard Radiation Oncology program in Boston, also states the real secret to survival (of a health challenge) may be "social support." Astoundingly, the study concluded that a strong system of mutual support was more helpful than chemotherapy for breast, prostate, colorectal and esophageal cancer as well.

If a HELPful support system can have this much of an impact on the epidemic of cancer, than I believe it is safe to assume that it would have a similar impact on any challenge, whether it was health related or not. I am living proof of that theory.

So what's the bad news? The bad news is what is going to happen to you if you don't apply the HELP philosophy® to your life? This next part may be really uncomfortable for you to hear. Brace yourself. If you don't become aware of your feelings about your situation and take the steps to move from HELPless to HELPful, then it is highly likely that you are going to remain a victim. Who would choose to be filled with the burning hurt of resentment and the despair of powerlessness for the rest of their lives? Who would elect a life of unrealized dreams and life unlived to it's full potential? The sad truth is that there are those, for whatever reason, that will choose this life. I am not as concerned as to why someone would choose this, then I am to wonder if you will be one of those people. I certainly hope not. I think it is proof positive that if you have stuck with me this far, you will choose to take the steps to HELPfulness.

Up until now it is possible you have been stewing in an environment filled with toxic messages about how powerless you are to take action and how being a victim is quite acceptable. Afterall, there's a government program for that, isn't there? And that asking for help meant you were weak and incapable. Now you know that bucket of lies no longer holds water.

Fortunately, someone who is feeling HELPless still has great power but they don't know it; very much like the elephant tied with a small rope to a stake since he was a baby, could now, as an adult, easily charge ahead. However, he does not realize he has this power. All he needs is to have someone show him the steps forward! I have shown you these steps.

BUT, how can I help someone else when I'm in so much pain? **BUT**, I have to figure out a solution for ME now. **BUT**, I can't possibly help someone else because I don't have any time to do what I have to do for me. **BUT,** I am desperate and on the verge of losing my business and my lifestyle I have worked so hard for. BUT? BUT? BUT? I've shouted similar protestations many times. You are not going to like what I am about to say; Do it anyway! The only thing standing in the way of you overcoming your challenge and realizing your solution is a big **BUT**. And a big **BUT** never did a thing for anyone.

Here's the real crux of what I figured out; you can't give HELP and be in tears and you can't give HELP and be yelling. Sure indicators you are laser focused on yourself. Hope, Encouragement, Love and Positivity can't exist in the same space as grief or outrage. Giving HELP somehow moves you mentally and emotionally to a more empowered place. At the very least, giving HELP gets you to a neutral place where you can better face your challenge and start to feel your power again.

Let me tell you as a friend and fellow human being dealing with daily life; a challenge does not have to call your character into question. Whether you respond to a challenge with what you feel is weakness or strength don't judge yourself. And for god sakes, don't judge others. We have to believe that we all are doing the best that we can.

No matter how you respond to your challenge initially, the HELP philosophy creates a level playing field from which you can find the HELPful person inside of you. Once on that level playing field you are in the game and available to make decisions wisely and comfortably and from a place of power and strength.

There will be some who read this book and have their doubts. And granted, my HELP Philosophy® may not be for everyone. You must decide for yourself. It would be wise to investigate the ramblings of a woman who has conked her noggin' twice and had visions of herself as a Mermaid at her wedding. Let's say I am full of malarkey; I have no clue as to what I am talking about and this whole book is Pollyanna protocol.

However, what if you just tried the HELP Philosophy® for one week?What if you were to change the way you have always faced your challenges for a month? What might it feel like to actually be prepared when the next challenge hits? How powerful would you feel if you knew exactly how to move through a crisis and help other people, as well as yourself without skipping a beat? What if you never had to get close to that place of overwhelming anger, frustration, grief and core shaking fear again? What if you never had to feel HELPless again? What do you have to lose?

If, for some outlandish reason, you couldn't make the HELP philosophy® work for you? Guess what? You will be no different than you are right now. So you have nothing to lose and perhaps realizing a fully activated life of your dreams to gain. You do it one step at a time as I have laid out before you.

I still apply the HELP Philosophy® to this day, in my own life as I continue to heal. I have found that I have a deep appreciation for all of the simple things that sometimes we look past in our everyday life. A simple pleasure for me now is to be able to walk across the room, reach high into the cupboard, select a glass, walk over to the refrigerator and pour the water into the glass. Do I run into the wall or bump into the table? Yes, many times I do. Do I ever miss the glass and flood the counter? Yes, on occasion I do. Do I ever break a glass? Of course! Do I celebrate my win, even if all those things happen in the course of me getting a drink of water? You bet I do! In order to be the HELPful person I know you want to be, let go of trying to be perfect and just do it. No matter how ugly it may look or the mess you might make. I have learned to embrace the fact that healing does not happen in a straight line and neither does life; some times there are some side steps along the way.

On April 14, 2012, on a white sandy beach on the west coast of Florida, I married the man of my dreams, TW Walker. In my custom mermaid wedding dress, I floated across sweet, sugary sand towards the heart TW had sculpted on the beach where he was waiting for me. Although family and friends surrounded us; TW's was the only face that I saw. I gently took step after step, one foot before the other, until finally I reached the hand of my beloved. On that spot I became a true Walker in action and in name. Can you imagine the joy of actually experiencing the moment you have seen a thousand times in your mind?

One of the ways I continue to celebrate overcoming my challenges and persevering is to keep reminders of my wedding day walk close to me. That is why I am usually wearing a replica of my wedding dress or something mermaid inspired when I speak to audiences, do book signings or make a television or even radio appearances. They serve as a great reminder of how far I have come.

Do you recall the great ad campaign for milk that asks "Got Milk?" I really like the imagination behind those ads and enjoy seeing them. What the ad is really driving at is to get people to stop and think if they have milk at home. Milk is a staple for most people; a necessity. Stealing the milk message I ask myself all the time, "Got Mermaid?" I even have a "Got Mermaid?" hat that I received as a gift from an audience member at a recent speaking engagement. I get mermaids all the time when I travel around speaking, signing books and teaching people the HELP philosophy®. They are some of my most cherished treasures.

Once you master the HELP philosophy® you will always be fully prepared to face the next challenge. Being prepared allows you to perform at your best under stressful confusing conditions that may veer you off course towards feeling HELPless. You build your support system by giving Hope, Encouragement, Love and Positivity.

When you master being HELPful it becomes an automatic response, like breathing. It allows you to build your support system, so that when a challenge arises for you, you can respond in a calm and confident manner knowing you are fully supported by those you have helped. I have given you the steps and strategies so you know how to become a master in the art of HELPfulness.

I have given you a formula for successful challenge recovery. Now, you know the precious secret. It's a power you have inside you called HELPability®

Don't keep it to yourself. Help me spread the word. Think of a world full of HELPful people making an impact on others. Be HELPful.

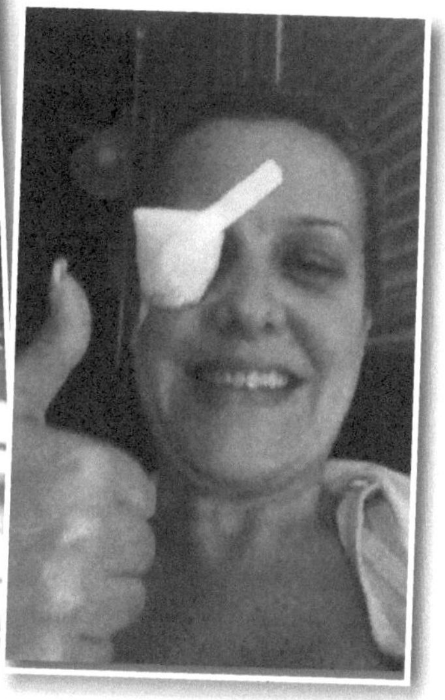

On our Honeymoon TW and I decided to first attend an event to get motivated.
Giving the thumbs up after one of my many eye surgeries to save my eyesight.

Message From TW Walker

I received "that" phone call. The call we all dread from the moment we first feel a connection with someone...our family, our friends, the ones we love. Someone is telling us there has been a terrible accident, and your loved one is injured. That sensation of panic burns white hot, racing through our bodies as we face one of life's most traumatic fears, the loss of someone we love. Napoleon Hill described this fear as the most painful of all the basic fears and the fear that can affect the mind so much as to cause permanent insanity.

On July 29th, 2011 I was notified that my fiancé Heather had fallen while at work. It was serious. After being air lifted to the Bayfront Trauma Center in St. Petersburg, Florida, she remained there for seven days unable to walk or function normally. She had suffered a traumatic brain injury, otherwise known as a TBI. After seven days there she was transferred to HealthSouth, a rehabilitation hospital in Sarasota where she spent the next four weeks going through intense physical and cognitive therapies just to regain basic physical and motor skills. Upon being released, I was charged with her care since I have a home office. There was no timetable for her recovery or if she would have a complete one.

Exactly ten days later, I was driving her back from a treatment she was receiving from a local acupuncturist when the unthinkable happened: at 40 mph a truck illegally turned in front of us and we collided. Within minutes paramedics were on the scene. Our vehicle was nearly totaled, and we were taken away by ambulance to a local hospital. There she was diagnosed with a second TBI, and nearly all progress she had made, was gone. I suffered a broken foot and also required back surgery.

The next several months were very trying for both of us as we fought to regain our former physical and mental selves, but it was during this time that we made the conscious decision that changes needed to happen; in my businesses and in our lives. And we did. Together we joined hearts and hands and said, "We're going to get through this and be stronger because of it!". She said words to me that still resonate with me today, "I believe it!".

We realized that life was too short to not do what you really want to do and live life to the fullest extent humanly possible.

I married Heather on April 14, 2012 in a lovely beach ceremony where she accomplished one of the major goals she set for herself while still in a wheelchair, when we decided that life was not going to stop us from charging forward: she walked down the sandy aisle unassisted. Although there's still a long road ahead for my wife, she has been one of my biggest inspirations.

Heather with Joel Osteen, Best Selling Author and American preacher, televangelist and the Senior Pastor of Lakewood Church, the largest Protestant Church in the United States.

Living the HELPful mission, here's Heather doing a 5K walk, raising money and awareness for pediatric cancer.

HELPFUL INSPIRATION

You Are Going To Want To Give Up...Get Up Instead

Challenges do not come with warning labels; be prepared with HELP.

— Heather O'Brien Walker

Are you feeling HELPful or HELPless in this moment?

— Heather O'Brien Walker

When you assume the opinions of others, you assume their lifestyle.

— TW Walker

No problem can be solved from the same level of consciousness that created it.

— Albert Einstein

Keep in mind that part of growing up is dealing with difficult issues, and the benefits can be great if you have the courage to ask for help. Human beings are not designed to go through life alone. No one has to bear the burden of tough times all by themselves.

— Jack Canfield

And so I wait. I wait for time to heal the pain and raise me to me feet once again – so that I can start a new path, my own path, the one that will make me whole again.

— Jack Canfield

It was not a tragedy that happened to me, it was a blessing.
— Joe Theisman

You can not, will not , nor ever hope to be a true success in life, if you think you are doing it by yourself
— Joe Theisman

I promise: Our whole purpose in life is just to make you happy!
— Famous Dave

May you always be surrounded by good friends and great barbeque.
— Famous Dave

Help others achieve their dreams and you will achieve yours.
— Les Brown

Just because Fate doesn't deal you the right cards, it doesn't mean you should give up. It just means you have to play the cards you get to their maximum potential.
— Les Brown

The secret to life is to have a task. Something that you devote your entire life too, something to bring everything to, every minute of the day for your whole life. And the important thing is, it must be something you can't possibly do.
— Henry Moore

Only a life lived for others is worthwhile.
— Albert Einstein

Refusing to ask for help when you need it is refusing someone the chance to be helpful.
— Ric Ocasek

Nothing liberates our greatness like the desire to help, the desire to serve.
— Marianne Williamson

Say and do something positive that will help the situation; it doesn't take any brains to complain.
— Robert A. Cook

All of us, at certain moments of our lives, need to take advice and to receive help from other people.
— Alexis Carrel

You have to accept whatever comes and the only important thing is that you meet it with courage and with the best that you have to give.
— Eleanor Roosevelt

When I do good, I feel good. When I do bad, I feel bad. That's my religion.
— Abraham Lincoln

Our prime purpose in this life is to help others. And if you can't help them, at least don't hurt them.
– Dalai Lama

We can't help everyone, but everyone can help someone.
– Ronald Reagan

Cherish your visions and your dreams as they are the children of your soul, the blueprints of your ultimate achievements.
— Napoleon Hill

About The Author

Heather O'Brien Walker started out as a quiet, shy Midwestern girl who had to pay someone to take her to her senior prom. However, having a family lineage of educators, diplomats and Pulitzer Prize winning journalists as role models, (her great grandfather being the president of the University of Michigan), she learned early on that perseverance and goal achievement was paramount to success.

After earning her degree in communications, one of her first positions was as a Franklin Covey business coach. She then advanced into a career as a cosmetics trainer for some of the world's leading cosmetic companies like Christian Dior, Lancôme, MAC, Trish Mc Evoy, The Body Shop and Chanel. This experience led her to become a key makeup artist and stylist behind many popular commercials for brand names like BF Goodrich, Ski-Doo, and Dodge, as well as feature films. She then became the personal assistant to A-list film actress, Demi Moore, then wife of Bruce Willis. This was where she learned all about the behind the scenes of Hollywood.

Heather continued on with her career to become a global hospitality consultant living in Europe and Tahiti while representing clients like Lufthansa, Bayer, and Louis Vuitton.

Now, as a Lifestyle Coach, author and inspirational speaker, she shares lessons from her life experiences and of overcoming adversity in the book Don't Give Up, Get Up! The book explains her unique HELP Philosophy® which helped her overcome her many obstacles. Heather is also creator of the HELPability® system for systematically overcoming adversities in life and business all based on this philosophy.

Heather is also the author of HELPability® Factor, which is a book and home study course based on her philosophy that helps people implement it to better face the challenges of doubt, fear, worry, and overwhelm in their daily lives.

Audiences and readers learn all about her heart wrenching experience of suffering two traumatic brain injuries in less than 40 days.

She was literally knocked down by a series of unbelievable circumstances and feeling helpless, with the privilege of walking, talking and caring for herself taken away from her temporarily. She shares how she fought through multiple adversities to achieve the goal of walking down the aisle to marry the man of her dreams that can help people overcome any challenge.

Made in United States
Troutdale, OR
08/04/2025

33410755R00070